20.70

D1178141

Alpine Club Guide Books

PENNINE ALPS EAST

PORTJENGRAT

ALPINE CLUB GUIDE BOOKS

Pennine Alps East

SAAS AND MISCHABEL CHAINS

companion volumes
Pennine Alps Central
Pennine Alps West

compiled and edited by

ROBIN G. COLLOMB

Alpine Club   London

PENNINE ALPS EAST
First published in Britain 1975 by
The Alpine Club London

Copyright © 1975 by West Col Productions

SBN 900523 13 1

Produced from computer information storage and retrieval
systems developed from volumes published under the title
Selected Climbs in the Pennine Alps (Neill) 1962 (one vol.)
Selected Climbs in the Pennine Alps (Collomb) 1968 (2 vols.)

Revised and re-written in three vols. as -
Pennine Alps East
Pennine Alps Central
Pennine Alps West

Designed, produced and sold for the Alpine Club by
West Col Productions
1 Meadow Close Goring Reading Berks. RG8 0AP

Set Olivetti Editor 5C typescript by Diana Gould
at West Col Productions

Printed offset in England by Swindon Press Ltd, Swindon, Wilts.

CONTENTS

INTERNATIONAL ALPINE DISTRESS SIGNAL

A more elaborate system of signals has been
devised in Britain but the International system
is basic to the subject of attracting attention
in an emergency.

Use a whistle, torch or flashes of the sun on
a mirror. Alternatively, shout, or wave
bright clothing:

Six regular flashes/notes in a minute, repeated
at intervals of a minute.

The reply is three signals per minute.

LIST OF DIAGRAMS AND ILLUSTRATIONS

Codes: PAE, PAC.

New information compiled from:
  Frischer-Roberts Diaries 1967, 1970, 1971, 1974
  A.K. Rawlinson reports 1970, 1971
  West Col Archives, Memoirs 1948, 1956, 1957, 1958, 1961, 1963,
  1964, 1967, 1971, 1974
  Correspondents' reports 1968-1974

Ground survey notes for Valtournanche-Valpelline South chain by:
  P. Charles and K. Rice, August 1974
  P. Charles and R.G. Collomb, August 1974
  R.G. Collomb and E. Roberts, September 1974
  Place Moulin-Prarayer, St. Barthélemy-Pierrey, Torgnon, Buisson,
  Valtournanche, Breuil

Photography and diagrams:
  Frischer-Roberts Archives 1961-1974
  West Col Archives 1946-1974
  Photographic processing: Ray Hebron and Photo Frischer

Text set Olivetti Editor 5C and IBM New Century verified at
West Col Productions by Diana Gould and Rosalind Stayne
Tapes 39A, 42C

Maps and technical publications mentioned in this guidebook are
available from Alpina Technica Productions 1 Meadow Close Goring
Reading Berks. RG8 0AP England

The previous guidebook to the Pennine Alps (Alpine Club, 1968) attempted to deal with the entire range in two volumes. This proved possible because large areas of ground at the eastern and western ends of the range were omitted or only covered by brief notes. In general throughout the entire length of the range, the Italian side received perfunctory treatment. This was partly due to economics in the amount of information that could be published, lack of first hand accounts and general ignorance of the Valpelline, Valtournanche and other Italian valleys. A lot of this can now be corrected but once again economics are the ruling force and only the most important information in mountaineering terms can be included where previously nothing had been published.

The result is a guidebook for the Pennine Alps in three volumes, of which the second and third are much larger than the first. The divisions of the range are now as follows:

I PENNINE ALPS EAST
Simplonpass to Monte Moropass and the Neues Weisstor
Weissmies, Portjengrat, Mischabel chains.

II PENNINE ALPS CENTRAL
Neues Weisstor to Col des Bouquetins
Monte Rosa, Matterhorn, Dent Blanche, Weisshorn
chains, Italian valley ranges, Valpelline South.

III PENNINE ALPS WEST
Col des Bouquetins to Col Ferret
Bouquetins, Grandes Dents chain, Collon-Pigne-Aiguilles
Rouges group, Cheilon-Ruinette group, Otemma-Valpelline
North, Grand Combin-Grand St. Bernard group.

To cope with this expansion valuable information has been supplied by over 200 correspondents, most of whom wrote unsolicited letters commenting on the 1968 edition. Letters received containing suggestions for a new edition number over 700. Several correspondents undertook to keep notes of visits to parts of the range unfrequented by British climbers, and the results of their work account for new or completely revised descriptions for 60 routes (Anthony Rawlinson, Eric Roberts, Jeremy Talbot).

An exhaustive edition of this guide to the Pennine Alps will probably never be published in English. But we may reasonably expect in the course of time to see a further improved edition with more complete coverage of the many sub-ranges and divisions of this magnificent part of the Alps.

Robin G. Collomb
Goring on Thames, July 1974

TECHNICAL SOURCE PUBLICATIONS CONSULTED

The undermentioned publications exclude journals and magazines and concern the complete Pennine Alps from Col Ferret to the Simplonpass. The date of publication/edition is shown in parenthesis.

Anderson, M. Mittel Switzerland. WCP (1974)

Ball, J. Ball's Alpine Guide: The Western Alps (1863, 1870, 1877, revised W. A. B. Coolidge, London, 1898)

Buscaini, G. Guida dei Monti d'Italia. Alpi Pennine. CAI/TCI.
   Vol I   Col du Petit Ferret to Col d'Otemma (1971)
   Vol II Col d'Otemma to Colle del Teodulo (1970)

Collomb, R. G. Selected Climbs in the Pennine Alps. AC (1968)
   Vol I   Saas Fee, Zermatt and Zinal.
   Vol II Arolla and Western ranges.

- Zermatt and district, including Saas Fee (London, 1969)

Conway, W. M. Climbers' Guide to the Central Pennine Alps (London, 1890)
   -            Climbers' Guide to the Eastern Pennine Alps (London, 1891)

Coolidge, W. A. B. Swiss Travel and Swiss Guide-books (London, 1889)

Dübi, H. Guide des Alpes Valaisannes, CAS (var. vols. 1919, 1922)

Kurz, M. Guide des Alpes Valaisannes, CAS
   Vol I   Col Ferret - Col Collon (1937, 1963, revised M. Brandt 1970)

   Vol II   Col Collon - Theodulpass (1930, 1947, revised M. Brandt 1970)
   Vol III Theodulpass - Simplon (1937)
   Vol IIIa Theodulpass - Monte Moro (1952, revised M. Brandt as Vol III, 1970)
   Vol IIIb Strahlhorn - Simplon (1952, revised M. Brandt as Vol IV, 1970)
   Vol IV   Simplon - Furka (1920)

Lunn, A. A History of Ski-ing (London, 1927)
           The Story of Ski-ing (London, 1953)

Pause, W. Im Schweren Fels (Munich, 1960)

Roberts, E. High Level Route, Chamonix-Zermatt-Saas. WCP (1973)

Saglio, S. Guida da rifugio a rifugio. Alpi Pennine. CAI (1951, 1954)
-                 I Rifugi del C.A.I. CAI (1957)

- & Boffa, F. Guida dei Monti d'Italia. Monte Rosa. CAI/TCI (1960)

Vanis, E. Im Steilen Eis (Munich, 1964)

Maps

Landeskarte der Schweiz (LK) 1:25,000. Normal grid sheets 1305, 1306, 1307, 1308, 1309, 1324, 1325, 1326, 1327, 1328, 1329, 1344, 1345, 1346, 1347, 1348, 1349, 1365, 1366 (1965-1974)

   1:50,000. Normal grid sheets 273, 274, 282, 283, 284, 285, 292, 293, 294 (1963-1973)

   1:50,000. District sheets 5003 (1968), 5006 (1972)

Istituto Geografico Militare (IGM), Carta d'Italia 1:25,000. Monte Cervino, carta speciale (1960)

   1:25,000. Normal grid sheets old series. Not consulted.

   1:50,000. New series normal grid sheets (series M792) 051, 069, 070, 071. None published at 31 December, 1973.

Carta delle zone turistiche d'Italia, Touring Club Italiano (TCI) 1:50,000 sheet No. 3 Il Cervino e il Monte Rosa (1965). No. 12 Gruppo del Monte Bianco (1968)

Kompass Wanderkarten (KK) 1:50,000. Sheet No. 85 Massiccio del Monte Bianco (1970), No. 87 Breuil-Cervinia-Zermatt (1972). Two unpublished sheets at 31 December 1973 covering the Pennine Alps East area are numbered 88 and 89.

12

SELECTED ENGLISH BIBLIOGRAPHY

A few volumes of general interest content are repeated from the source publications listed on the previous page.

Ball, J. Peaks, Passes and Glaciers (First Series). 1859

Ball, J. The Alpine Guide: Western Alps. 1898 Coolidge ed.

Clark, R.W. The Early Alpine Guides. 1949

-                The Victorian Mountaineers. 1953

-                The Day the Rope Broke. 1965

-                The Alps. 1973

Collomb, R.G. Alpine Points of View. 1961

-                Zermatt and district. 1969

Conway, W.M. The Zermatt Pocket Book. 1881

Coolidge, W.A.B. The Alps in Nature and History. 1908

-                Alpine Studies. 1912

Dent, C.T. Above the Snow Line. 1887

Field & Spencer. Peaks, Passes and Glaciers (Third Series). 1932

Finch, G.I. The Making of a Mountaineer. 1924

Gos, C. Alpine Tragedy. 1948

Gos, F. Zermatt and its Valley. 1926

Kennedy, E.S. Peaks, Passes and Glaciers (Second Series). 2 vols. 1862

Klucker, C. Adventures of an Alpine Guide. 1932

Lunn, A. Zermatt and the Valais. 1955

-                A Century of Mountaineering. 1957

Moore, A.W. The Alps in 1864. 2 vols. Blackwell ed. 1939

Mummery, A.F. My Climbs in the Alps and Caucasus, republished 1974

Norman-Neruda, L. The Climbs of Norman-Neruda. 1899

Pilley, D.E. Climbing Days. 2nd ed. 1965

Ratti, A.A. Climbs on Alpine Peaks. 1928

Rébuffat, G. Starlight and Storm. 1955

-                Men and the Matterhorn. 1967

Roch, A. Climbs of My Youth. 1949

Rey, G. The Matterhorn. Blackwell ed. 1946

Scott, D. Big Wall Climbing. 1974

Smythe, F.S. Edward Whymper. 1940

Stephen, L. The Playground of Europe. Blackwell ed. 1936

Tyndall, J. Hours of Exercise in the Alps. 1871

Whymper, E. Scrambles Among the Alps in the Years 1860-69. 6th ed. 1936

-              Zermatt and the Matterhorn. 1897, republished 1974

Williams, C. Zermatt Saga. 1964

Wills, A. Wandering Among the High Alps. Blackwell ed. 1939

Young, G.W. On High Hills. 5th ed. 1947

-              Mountains with a Difference. 1951

ABBREVIATIONS

AACZ	Zürich University Alpine Club
AC	Alpine Club
Aig.	Aiguille
Biv.	Bivouac
c.	approximately
CAAI	Italian Universities Alpine Club
CAI	Italian Alpine Club
CAS	Swiss Alpine Club
Gr.	German
h.	hour(s)
IGM	Italian military map
Ital.	Italian
Kl.	Klein(e)
km.	kilometre(s)
L	left (direction)
LK	Swiss federal map
m.	metre(s)
min.	minute(s)
mtn.	mountain
P, Pta.	Pizzo, Punta
pt.	point (spot height)
Pte.	Pointe (summit)
R	right (direction)
SAC	Swiss Alpine Club
TCI	Italian Touring Club
U.	Unter
WCP	West Col Productions
*	asterisk against an altitude signifies an approximate height, or a height either ascertained from an Italian source or from a foreign publication.
25m.	1:25,000 map (e.g. LK25, LK25m.)
50m.	1:50,000 map (e.g. LK50, LK50m.)

Compass directions are indicated as: N, S, E, W, NE, SW, etc.

Introduction

In the opening remarks to the 1968 edition reference was made to the number of changes which had taken place in the valleys since the 1962 edition had been published; also to the proliferation of mechanical methods of gaining height in the mountains. During the past seven years fewer changes of this nature can be recorded but in some cases they are significant enough to modify the mountaineering aims and instincts of visitors. These changes have been recorded in comments and descriptions embodied in the guide.

Mountaineering is now such an expensive pastime even compared with ten years ago that no purpose is served by giving an indication of costs, or advice on how to travel to the numerous centres in such a diverse area like the Pennine Alps. At the present time all the main centres can be reached by road (except Zermatt village), and where railheads exist these are mentioned in descriptions. Access by helicopters is still a small business (but it would be foolish to predict that it might remain that way), and the irony of many flying journeys is that they are made by climbers to landing pads beside huts above the snowline. For the first time the system of goodwill and reciprocal arrangements over charges made in huts to climbers was put under great strain due to economic factors in 1973. Whereas some order has been restored the future of the system as it has been known for decades between various Alpine counries is likely to remain unsettled, and climbing parties should be prepared to pay more than the rates they believe they are entitled to. In Switzerland the only sure way of securing maximum reductions is to prove membership of the Swiss Alpine Club. In Italy charges are generally higher, certainly more erratic, so that you might stay at one hut for next to nothing and pay exorbitantly at the next; with luck it averages out.

MAPS

The guide is designed for use with the official Swiss map (LK). Wherever possible descriptions are based on consultation with the new grid series on a scale of 1:25,000. The older 1:50,000 map is still being updated by LK, and gradually the variation in heights especially but also other information is being incorporated from the 1:25,000 map. Annoyingly, some information of value to mountaineers appearing on the 1:50,000 map does not appear on the 1:25,000. The Swiss maps extend right across the crest zone of the range into Italy so that in general the official Italian map (IGM, pre-1939 in surveying) has not been consulted. A new IGM map of 1:50,000 is scheduled to be published in a few years (see Technical Source Publications Consulted). The following LK maps refer to the entire Pennine Alps range:

1:25,000 grid series

1287	Sierre	1325	Sembrancher	1347	Matterhorn
1288	Raron	1326	Rosablanche	1348	Zermatt
1289	Brig	1327	Evolène	1349	Monte Moro
1306	Sion	1328	Randa	1365	Gd. St. Bernard
1307	Vissoie	1329	Saas	1366	M. Velan
1308	St. Niklaus	1345	Orsières	1367	Valtournanche
1309	Simplon	1346	Chanrion	1368	Gressoney

A special district map of Saas Fee, consisting of parts of sheets 1328, 1329, 1348, 1349, was issued in 1972 by the Saas Fee Verkehrsverein. Ref: KF 0740. It shows ski routes and emphasises paths, cableways, etc. with additional colours.

1:50,000 grid series

273	Montana	282	Arolla	292	Courmayeur
274	Visp	284	Mischabel	293	Valpelline
282	Martigny	285	Domodossola	294	Gressoney

1:50,000 district series

5003 Mont Blanc - Grand Combin   5006 Zermatt und
                                        Umgebung

1:100,000 grid series

41   Col du Pillon   46 Val de Bagnes
42   Oberwallis   47 Monte Rosa

Water-resistant syntosil versions of some of the 50m. and
25m. maps are available with ski routes shown; they cost
nearly double the price of regular sheets. Warning: prices
of maps given in the 1968 edition of the guide have more than
doubled in terms of British money.

ALTITUDES AND NOMENCLATURE

All heights are taken from the LK25 map. Where the map does
not show an altitude, it has been ascertained from an Italian
source, or from a calculation from contour lines on the map.
These cases are marked with an asterisk (*). The height given
in graded climbing is the vertical distance from the base of a
route to its summit (not necessarily the summit of the parent
mtn.), and always excludes the height gained in approaching
the climb, say from a hut.

Place names are taken generally from the LK25 map. Excep-
tions are traditional names in popular use which have been
changed on the latter map. In these cases the map name appears in parenthesis. Many changes in the spelling of place
names on LK25 are due to the adoption of dialectical pronun-
ciation which translates into major variations of spelling.
These will confuse climbers for another generation and have
already been severely criticised by mountaineering authorities
in Switzerland. But the deed has now been done.

French, German and Italian names for climbing routes have
been chosen according to popular British usage. These are
sometimes an admixture of English and another language. It
is appreciated that the choice is arbitrary, and the names

believed to be widely understood by British climbers are used. Some have been changed from the 1968 edition of the guide. Thus Younggrat rather than Klein Triftjigrat; Viereselsgrat rather than Arête des Quatre Anes. In this choice German versions predominate, giving way to French as one moves to the W, or to Italian on the frontier ridge.

ORIENTATION

The directions left (L) and right (R) in the sense of direction of movement of the climber - ascent, descent, traverse of slope - have been used consistently throughout. For mountain features such as glaciers, couloirs, rivers, etc. the traditional orographical reference to left and right banks as viewed in the direction of flow, i.e. downward, has been abandoned, due to the number of complaints received over the confusion this system causes. These features are therefore now described in the sense of movement of the climber. For example, you go up the L side of a glacier, which was previously described as ascending the R bank. In some descriptions both ways are given to emphasise orientation. Compass directions are also given to assist route finding.

WINTER AND SKI ASCENTS

Following decades of disagreement on the validity of winter ascents according to dates recorded, a recent UIAA recommendation that the period for counting winter ascents should run from 21 December to 20 March has met with disfavour in some quarters; doubtless general adoption of this period would eliminate many claims to notable first winter ascents made up to 15 April, sometimes later. Without wishing to enter into the argument, in this guide dates from 21 December to 31 March are admitted as winter ascents. The guide also reports important ascents on ski at any time of the year. The contemporary "sport" of "extreme ski", being the descent of snow and ice faces on ski, is recorded for appropriate routes.

CAMPING

There are official campsites with good facilities including shops at the following base centres. Their locations are not always obvious and are generally on the outskirts of villages. If in doubt consult the local tourist bureau, normally found in the centre of a village.

Arolla (poor facilities), Breuil, Gressoney-St. Jean, Les Haudères, Macugnaga, Randa, St. Niklaus, Saas Fee, Saas Grund, Täsch, Zermatt, Zinal.

GRADING OF CLIMBS

In accordance with the UIAA classification system, the grading of rock climbs is numerical from I to VI and A1, A2, A3 and A4 for artificial, with the letter 'e' to denote the use of expansion bolts (e.g. A3e). Grade I is the easiest and VI the hardest. Variations of difficulty are denoted by + and - signs; plus is above the normal rating and minus below (i.e. V-/V/V+). These variations above Grade IV will matter for the expert climber, and they should be equally helpful in the lower grades for the average performer. It must be stressed that the grade of a climb is determined not only by pure technical difficulty but also by objective danger and length.

Mixed climbs and snow/ice climbs are also graded in six stages. This grading is always more approximate and less precise than the numerical rock grades because of variable conditions in a season and from year to year. Winter climbing will be different again, and apart from severe cold grades could be lower or higher according to the nature of the route. In order of rising difficulty: F (easy), PD (moderately difficult), AD (fairly difficult), D (difficult), TD (very difficult),

ED (extremely difficult). Further refinement is possible by adding plus or minus signs.

The previous guide elaborated on this subject at great length, and went a good deal further by introducing classifications for the sustained nature of routes, and for their relative steepness. While only praise was penned about this treatment, it is felt that climbers must rely on more comprehensive information given in route preambles for these subtleties, and the classifications given for them in the previous guide are now omitted.

MOUNTAINEERING TERMS, LANGUAGE AND GLOSSARY

For the most part terms used in this guide, though not always proper English words, will be known and understood to alpinists. The subject has grown in complexity due to new techniques and slang phrases emerging mainly from the English, French, German and Italian languages. (One ignores just as many coming from modern American mountaineering which no editor would dare apply to descriptions of an Alpine region!). A dictionary of such terms cross referenced in English, Americanese, French, German and Italian is in preparation by Robin Collomb and Eric Roberts for publication in 1975.

Valley bases

SIMPLONPASS - SIMPLON VALLEY - VAL DIVEDRO

The main approaches into the area from the E side lead from the Simplon road pass. Buses from Brig to summit, 5 times a day; continuing to Simplon Dorf (village), 4 times; and to Domodossola, twice daily. From Brig:

22.5 km. <u>Simplon Kulm</u> (summit, 2005m.). Bellevue hotel on summit, two others a short way down on S side. Car park, camping possible. One ski tow. No food purchase. See also Simplonpass entry in Part I.

31.7 km. <u>Simplon Dorf</u> (village, 1476m.). Small, prosperous, German-Speaking community. Hôtel de la Poste, plain but good accommodation. Two other hotels. Limited car parking. Camping possible. Good food shop. Starting point for Laggin bivouac.

41.6 km. <u>Gondo</u> (Rüden - Gr.) (855m.). Small breezy resort at lower entrance to Gondo Gorge. Hotels, pensions, shops, bank, camping. Starting point for excursions up the Zwischbergen valley.

63.1 km. <u>Domodossola</u> (270m.). Important Italian town, hot and dusty in summer, the starting point for approaches to Antronapiana and Macugnaga. Buses for all destinations depart from the station forecourt. Timetables in station booking hall and on the wall of café across forecourt: Autoservizi Comazzi. Direct rail connections to Arona, Milan, Turin, or back to Brig through the Simplon tunnel.

VALLE D'ANTRONA - ANTRONAPIANA

Geographically an important base centre for the Italian side of the Pennines East area, but in fact rarely visited by anyone except local Domodossola climbers. The valley opens at Villa-dossola, 7 km. S of Domodossola. Bus service three times a day from Domodossola station forecourt (see above) to <u>Antron-apiana</u> (908m.). This is a large village/resort where the valley divides: hotels, shops, etc. Motor roads continue up the branch valleys (no bus service, taxis available) to <u>Alpe Cheggio</u> hamlet and the Cavalli barrage (1490m.), and to the Campliccioli barrage (1352m.). CAI hut at former hamlet (q. v. Novara), which is the main approach to all climbing in the Andolla basin.

VALLE ANZASCA - MACUGNAGA

This valley, leading from below Domodossola and Viladossola to one of the most important mountaineering centres in the Alps, is not really a legitimate base for excursions in the Pennines East area. It is however the point from which you start to cross the Monte Moro pass. As this is now rapidly becoming one of the most popular walking routes in the Pennines, after decades of casual visits, the valley must be included. Five buses a day from Domodossola station forecourt (see above), journey time $1\frac{1}{2}$ h.

<u>Macugnaga</u> (34 km. from Domodossola) is formed by three village/hamlets: Borca, Staffa, Pecetto. Staffa (1307m.) is the largest and main centre, picturesque and plainly a tourist para-dise. Hotels, pensions, shops, garages, tourist office and guides' bureau, camping. Cableway to Monte Moro pass (q. v.). Cableways from Pecetto (1362m.) to the Belvedere and Alpe Rosareccio. Many more skilifts and tows. Macugnaga enjoys a bigger reputation in winter. Apart from public transport and cableways (marginally) all costs at Macugnaga in 1971 were found to be similar to those at Zermatt and Saas.

SAAS VALLEY

One of the best known valleys in the Western Alps. From Visp in the Rhone valley (rail and bus services) you first reach Stalden where the valley divides: the W branch goes up to Zermatt, the E to Saas. Post bus service from Stalden to Saas Fee about eight times a day, with additional services running from Brig via Visp to Saas Fee without stopping at Stalden. Supplementary services at peak times. From Saas Grund, just below Saas Fee, a separate local service continues higher up the valley to the Mattmark barrage, eight times a day. The main centre of Saas Fee itself is situated on a shelf above the valley bed on the W (Mischabel) side.

From Brig:

Visp (663m.). Main line railway and bus services.

Stalden (809m.). Mountain railway (Zermatt) and bus services.

Saas Balen (1487m.). Bus services. The least popular of the Saas resorts, pleasant and comparatively quiet, main road bypasses village centre. Simple facilities. Normal exit point for reaching Simplonpass by high level walking routes.

Saas Grund (1559m.). 32 km. Main centre in the valley bottom, at junction with road up to Saas Fee. Good facilities and services. Campsite. Important cableway to the Triftalp (2300m.*). Main departure point for the Weissmies chain.

Saas Fee (1790m.). 37 km. from Brig. The main centre in this valley, all kinds of shops, pensions, hotels, public services, etc. Tourist office, guides' bureau, extensive cableway systems. Cars must be left in the compound on outskirts of village (parking fee). Departure point for many ascents on E side of the Mischabel chain. Important ski resort in winter.

Saas Almagell (1673m.). 36 km. The charming upper village in the valley. Good facilities, tourist office and bank. Private campsite. Departure point for the Portjengrat and Sonniggrat climbs.

Mattmark barrage café (2180m.*). 43 km. Bus terminus. The café is marked but not named on current map. The final part of the road ascends diagonally across the face of the dam and ends on reaching its head at the W end. The terminus is slightly below this point. Between the café and the roadhead the extensive verges form a public car park. Cars must not be taken either along the rough road across the top of the dam or into the continuation galleries forming a road for lorries along the W side of the barrage. There is no accommodation at the Mattmark bus terminus, but an inn has been opened at the S end of the barrage, 45 min. on foot by the lorry road along the W side of the lake towards the Monte Moro pass, at pt. 2238m.

ZERMATT VALLEY

See also introduction to Saas valley above. This is the W branch of the two valleys which join at Stalden, above Visp in the Rhone valley. The rack railway follows this valley to Zermatt. Post bus service to St. Niklaus. Above this point the motor road may now be used by the public up to Täsch (large carpark), the last village below Zermatt. The continuation road is reserved for residents of Zermatt. Trains up and down the valley about 12 times a day.

From Brig:
Visp (663m.). Main line railway and bus services.

Stalden (809m.). Mountain railway and bus services. Junction with Saas valley.

St. Niklaus (1127m.). Mountain railway and bus services.

Randa (1407m.). 34 km. Railway and public road. Shops, hotels, post office, bank, etc. Schools holiday centre. Private camping. Departure point for Dom, Täschhorn, Weisshorn, etc.

<u>Täsch</u> (1438m.). 38 km. Railway and public road terminus. Large carpark. Shops, hotels, post office, etc. Campsite. Taxi service to Täschalp. Departure point for Täschhorn-Rimpfischhorn sector of Mischabel chain.

<u>Zermatt</u> (1606m.). 44 km. from Brig. Railway terminus. All main services, supermarkets. Main campsite situated 400m. below station on main road away from village. There are other private campsites. Youth hostel on the outskirts at the hamlet called Obere Steinmatte (Winkelmatten-Findeln road). English and French widely spoken. All inquiries can be dealt with at the tourist bureau adjoining the station. Station for rack railway to Gornergrat almost opposite main station. Cableway station terminii are some distance from railway station and a town plan is invaluable for finding the way round this complex resort. In winter one of the premier ski resorts of the Western Alps.

Section One

SIMPLONPASS - MONTE MOROPASS

Huts and other mountain bases

<u>Simplonpass hotels</u> 2005m.

See Simplonpass entry in Part I of the guide.

<u>Laggin Bivouac</u> 2746m.

Bivouac du Laggin. Now shown on map. CAS property. Situated below the foot of the SE ridge of the Fletschhorn, on a small grass and rock promontory forming the first step on the preliminary ridge rising above pt. 2687. 9m. (LK50). An aluminium building in one compartment, opened in 1959, with 12 dortoir places in two tiers, blankets, etc. Wood stove, cooking and eating utensils complete. Wood store, water source and toilet outside. No warden, door unlocked.

1. Frequent red waymarks all the way. From Simplon Dorf (village, 1476m.), pass through the archway dividing the Poste hotel, opposite the bus stop, and take the path uphill then in a rising traverse over pasture, across a stream in a deep-cut bed and into the forest, up to the Wäng chalets (1620m.). Continue in the open, then in forest, alternately, making height quickly, and finally climb a series of zigzags to the corner called Bärenfad (2059. 2m.) where the path turns into the Laggintal, narrows and becomes slightly overgrown ($1\frac{1}{2}$ h.). Small shrine. The path now takes a rising and falling line across a steep grassy headwall (Goldwäng), high above the Laggintal, then climbs in short steep zigzags to pt. 2195m. and a commemorative cross. In a few m. it crosses the head of a small grassy gully and a large red arrow on a stone points R (45 min.). (The path continues to the sheep enclosures called Feriche - 2175m., which is a lower and incorrect line for the hut; no waymarks). Above the path, climb pleasant grass slopes in a rising traverse above Feriche, in parts trackless but always with frequent red flashes on stones. Cross a small grassy headland, then a few boulders, and climb a low rockband into a shallow grassy valley with large rocks. From the head of this go out slightly R on to an old moraine and climb to a headland with conspicuous cairn on L (2422.5m.). Avoid this by keeping R and cross the last grassy trough to reach the true R lateral moraine of the Zibelenfluh glacier. Follow the moraine crest over pt. 2506m. and continue to a point where a slight descent is made over blocks; the hut is seen a short distance above. In the small depression below a huge landslide has caused the moraine crest to disappear in a crumbling wall; in 1971 it was advisable to give this place a wide berth on the R. Return to the crest and follow it to a traverse L (not far below the moraine top), leading to the promontory and the hut ($2\frac{1}{4}$ h., $4\frac{1}{2}$ h. from Simplon village).

Weissmies Hut 2726m.

Weissmieshütte. CAS property. A large building situated on a grassy terrace below a series of moraines under the Trift glacier and directly opposite (SE of) the Jägigrat. Warden and restaurant/hotel service, places for 110. The most popular mtn. venue in this area.

2. From Saas Grund (1559m.) follow the main road N to a sign-post on the R at houses called Gasse. Take a lane parallel with the road to the houses of Unter dem Berg (1569m.), then start up the large mule path which zigzags in meadow then in the Trift forest to the Trift hamlet, inn (2072m.). Continue along the unmistakeable path, now more or less under the cableway, to the Kreuzboden chalets (2397m., Chrizboden, LK25), and finally go up directly to the hut ($2\frac{3}{4}$ h. from Grund).

The new Trift cableway reduces the approach on foot to 1 h. Cableway station lies on main road 150m. beyond Gasse. From the terminus at 2300m. descend about 20m. to a traverse path running NW from a building at 2283m. Take this traverse to the mule path which is reached above the cowsheds at 2281m., and not far below Kreuzboden.

Almagelleralp Hotel 2194m.

An old building on a popular and pleasant site directly above Saas Almagell. It lies in the side valley E of the village, and belongs to the village commune. Accommodation is now in rooms with beds (single, double or treble). Moderate rates, good cuisine. The cableway (for passengers or luggage) is inoperative at present.

3. Start either from the main village square, opposite tourist office, and work directly through small houses to the path rising N at first into the forest. Or, from the communal carpark beside the disused cableway station on the main road at the N end of the village, from where the path goes up near the stream to join the first one in the forest. A series of pleasant zigzags in the forest lead to a bridge, whence a straight section on the L side of the stream goes directly to the hotel; ignore a fork L at the Stafel cowsheds ($1\frac{1}{4}$-$1\frac{1}{2}$ h. from Almagell).

The Furggstalden chairlift, from the S end of the village, to 1900m. is of no advantage, as the traversing path to join the hotel trail descends a considerable distance in the forest.

Novara Hut 1465m.*

Rifugio Città di Novara. Not marked on map. CAI property. Situated on the lower outskirts of the hamlet of Alpe Cheggio, at the roadhead above Antronapiana (908m.). Access from the latter resort by small road, or by footpath with shortcuts (2 h.). Warden and restaurant service, places for 56.

Andolla Hut 2052m. 2061m. IGM

Rifugio d'Andolla: formerly "Edison hut". CAI property.

Marked on LK 25. A small building situated on a grassy headland a short distance S of the Andolla Alp chalets (2038m.), above the bed of the Loranco valley; this valley is called colloquially the "Andolla basin". It gives access to the best and least frequented climbing in the Pennine East area on the Italian side of the mtns. 18 dortoir places, small equipped kitchen. Wood scarce, so take your own stove. Door found unlocked in 1971, but it is believed locked at times; keys at Novara hut.

4. From the Novara hut (see above) go through the hamlet of Alpe Cheggio and up to the dam wall of the Cavalli barrage (1490m.) in a few min. Cross the top of the dam to the S end and continue along a good path above the SW side of the barrage, to its far end. The path descends to a bridge across the Loranco stream (1495m.). Ignore this and continue above the L side of the stream to a second bridge. Cross this and follow a path on the R side to the Ronchelli chalets (1578m.). After reaching a small shrine the path divides. Keep L, near the valley bed, then rise gradually above it, till another fork is reached, not far short of the Campolamana chalets (1721m.). Take the R branch, uphill, in large zigzags, and by keeping to the main path L at small junctions reach the Andolla Alp chalets (2038m.). Climb to the upper group of chalets among large rocks on the pasture, then turn L (W and S) along a traverse path, cross a stream in a hollow with a waterfall below, and so reach the hut ($3\frac{1}{2}$ h. from Novara hut).

<u>Malnate Hut</u> 2796m. *

Rifugio Città di Malnate. Replaces the former Bionda hut, on another site close by. The new hut was formerly the customs house. CAI property. A comfortable hut with electricity and gas cooking, situated 5 min. scramble away to the E of the upper terminus of the Macugnaga-Monte Moropass cableway (from where the building cannot be seen). Follow signs to the N then E (2-3 min.) and turn sharp R (SE) down a hidden rock staircase with handrail. Warden and restaurant service, places for 30. For the route on foot from Macugnaga (approx. 4 h.), see Monte Moropass. The path follows a rocky trough somewhat below and

E of the hut (i. e. even further from the cableway), and about 15 min. from the top of the pass. The hut seems to be used mainly by Macugnaga tourists for catching an early morning view of the famous E face of Monte Rosa, and by walking parties crossing the pass.

Mattmark Inn 2238m.

Private property. A small, new inn was under construction in 1971. It is connected to the jeep road at the S end of the Mattmark barrage by an access lane.

PART I

Weissmies chain

Simplonpass to Zwischbergenpass

5. SIMPLONPASS 2005m.

Italian: Colle Sempione. The great division between the Penine Alps and Lepontine Alps. The pass of the Simplon is the lowest of the great passes across the main range of the Alps between the Montgenevre and the Lukmanier.

The broad summit plateau (Simplon Kulm) is all pasture and lies between the Monte Leone massif and grassy summits at the N end of the Weissmies chain. From the usual viewpoints the actual summit of Monte Leone cannot be seen. Beyond the Hospice the Rossboden face of the Fletschhorn stands out well. On the highest point of the pass stands the Bellevue hotel (post bus stop), with kiosk, skitow and public carpark. This hotel is noted for its comfort and cuisine. 300m. further along the road is a smaller hotel with good facilities, and after passing the Hospice building, a third hotel lies about 500m. towards Simplon Dorf.

There is no official campsite but many suitable sites. The Hospice will give shelter to students and youth parties. The ascent of Monte Leone and other summits in the group are described in Mittel Switzerland (West Col, 1974). Frequent bus service from Brig, 22.5 km. No food purchase. Brig to Domodossola, 63 km.

BISTINE(N)PASS 2416m.
SIMELIPASS 3022m.

In combination these two passes connect the easiest walking route from the Simplon to the Saas valley. The latter is a rough crossing and may be found snow covered till mid August. F.

6. From the Simplon Kulm (Belvedere Hotel) go along the main road for over 1 km., to a signposted path on the R, leading to the Blatten chalets. This path is well marked all the way to the Bistinenpass. After the chalets it makes a rising traverse SW across pastures, then continues up grassy slopes due W to the col (2h.).

On the other side (Nanztal) descend past two small tarns to a vague traverse path. Turn L(SW) along this and follow it by contouring round the Magenhorn and Galenhorn. Under the latter the path has gained a little height and forks. Keep R and descend gradually to the small gorge at the head of the Nanztal. (The L branch goes up to the Sirwoltensattel - see below). Climb along the top of the gorge, cross the stream descending through it and work up the L side of large hillock pt. 2507.5m. Above this climb the scree and rock bed of the cwm leading to the Simelipass. There is nearly always snow in the top part of this N side of the col (3½h., 5½h. from Simplon Kulm).

On the other side (Mattwald valley) descend rough slopes SSW, and lower down cross two irrigation channels as the pastures are reached. Continue down the true R side of the valley to c. 2450m. Now cross the main stream L and make an horizontal traverse WSW under the rock face marked by pt. 2731.7m. Continue almost due W down to the large grassy hump of Siwiboden, and reach a well-marked path just above the large cairned pt. 2172. 4m. Follow the path SE to the Siwinen huts (2077m.), then descend R through the woods in large zigzags to Saas Balen (2½h. in descent from Simelipass, 8h. from Simplon Kulm).

SIR WOLTE(N)SATTEL 2621m.

This saddle is the second depression S of the Bistinenpass in the grassy ridge enclosing the W side of the Simplon depression. Assuming one can use transport on the S side of the Simplon, by crossing this saddle a somewhat shorter, more interesting, but hardly quicker connection is provided in combination with the Simelipass, to the Saas valley. In fact, this route is the classic way, and the combination was first done by a tourist party on 8 July, 1863: A. W. Moore with Melchior Anderegg.

7. From the Simplon Kulm go down the main road S, by bus or car, to the house of Engiloch (1791m.), on L side of road (authorised bus stop). On foot, 4 km., about 45 min.

Return up the road for 300m., and take a path on the L, over the river and up to the Klusmatten chalets (1823m.). Follow a good path going up the grassy slopes on the L side of the stream, to reach a small plateau called Weissboden. Continue closer to the stream, up to the foot of a rock barrier below an upper lake-filled cwm. Climb the barrier by a scree gangway slanting up from left to right (well indicated on map) and finish above the head of the conspicuous waterfall in the barrier. Cross the stream and work up W round the N side of a smaller barrier below the lake marked pt. 2437m. Continue climbing W, away from and above the lake, directly towards the obvious saddle, on the R side of a stream bed, and finally work somewhat R(NW) up grass and scree to the col (3h. from Engiloch, 3¾h. from Simplon Kulm on foot)

On the other side (Nanztal) descend by a path for a few min., and when it starts to bend round R(N), leave it. Make a rough but short traverse L(SW) and join the previous route near the small stream gorge at the head of the Nanztal. Then as for Route 6 to the Simelipass ($2\frac{1}{2}$h. from Sirwoltensattel). Allow 8h. from Engiloch to Saas Balen, and an extra hour if walking to former starting point from Simplon Kulm.

BÖSHORN 3267.6m.

The first snow mtn. at the N end of the Weissmies chain. Alternative name: Rauthorn. Infrequently climbed, fine regional view. By S ridge from Rossbodenpass (q.v.) in about 1h., keeping L to avoid gendarmes (F+). By E ridge reached from N side (Sirwolten lakes), interesting, 3h. from head of rock barrier/waterfall on Route 7, F+. First ascent not traced.

ROSSBODE(N)PASS 3169m.

Between the Böshorn and Sengkuppe, an old glacier pass from Simplon Dorf (Village) to the Saas valley. Less frequented today, but fine and recommended. The lowest pt. of the pass is a few m. below and to the N of the exact place of the regular crossing, at the head of the big E-side couloir. First tourist traverse: M. Viridet, E. Boissier and G.F. Reuter with M. Zurbriggen, 1 August, 1833.
  E side, F+. W side, F.

8. E side. From Simplon Village go up the main road of the pass to Eggen hamlet (1588m.). 2km., 30 min. on foot. Follow lane between the houses which leads to a path going SW up a wooded spur to reach on the pastures Rossboden hamlet (1932m.). Leave the huts by working up slopes to the N, in zigzags, then go W at a fork, continuing steeply but on a good track to a rock barrier below pt. 2348m. Climb this by a rising traverse L (marked) and cross a large hump (2225m.) to reach the Griessernen cwm by a slight descent. Follow a track in the cwm on a grassy spur then on a moraine crest, up to the SE foot of the Böshorn at pt. 2669m. Move L on to the Griessernen glacier, and climb it over a short distance and with a few crevasses to the foot of the big couloir descending the E side of the col. (In favourable conditions, the lower part of the couloir gives good glissading in descent). Cross the foot of the couloir and make a rising traverse L on to the broken rock rib enclosing it on the S side. Climb easy rocks and scree up this rib, with traces of a track, to the ridge and col (4h. from Simplon Village).

9. W side. From Saas Balen take the steep forest path due E, to the Brand chalets (1959m.). Continue on the path first N then SE and N again in zigzags, up to the Gruben huts (2301m.) (2h.). From here take a small track up the R side of the stream coming down from the Gruben glacier. This peters out on reaching moraines below the glacier, but there are cairns. Cross the stream bed L and follow moraines up to a promontory, behind which is a small tarn (2780m.). (An alternative route to the tarn keeps R and takes the lower tongue of the glacier). Continue up the L side of the Gruben glacier, on snow patches, ice and moraine, passing R of a tiny tarn at pt. 2854m. Now move L and climb rough grass and rock slopes with a faint track, towards the ridge of the Rothorngrat. It is reached at a snowy saddle (3135m.), marking the E end of the Rothorngrat and the continuation ridge rising to the Sengkuppe. On the other (N) side cross the snow slopes of the Mattwald glacier, making a horizontal traverse to the col, crevasses possible (6h. from Saas Balen).

Note: From the Weissmies hut there is a traversing route towards the col, round slopes below the Jägihorn, then up to the lower tongue of the Gruben glacier, where the approach from the valley is joined. The track round the Jägihorn is in poor condition. Well marked on map (Weissmies hut to pass, $4\frac{1}{2}$h.).

SENGKUPPE (SENGGCHUPPA) 3606m.

No name on LK50 map. A prominent shoulder and step in the main ridge of the Weissmies chain, above the Rossbodenpass, preceding the summit mass of the Fletschhorn. No merit in itself.

FLETSCHHORN 3993m.

The most complex mtn. in this guidebook area, and one of the most important from the climbing point of view. It provides almost an equal amount of snow/ice and rock climbing, but the latter is less important because it frequently degenerates into mixed terrain which is serious enough except in very dry conditions. Recent ascents of the N face confirm that this is one of the finest summits in the Swiss Alps.
  The summit ridge, horseshoe in shape with the open end facing SW, causes the main ridge of the Weissmies chain to make a meandering loop. The mtn. is frequently traversed round this horseshoe to the Lagginhorn in a pleasant outing from the Weissmies hut. Coming up from the Rossbodenpass, over the Sengkuppe, the horseshoe is reached precisely at the culminating point (3993m.). This arm of the loop descends towards the Weissmies hut. The main ridge swings E then S, first to a high saddle (3904m.) then to pt. 3919m., which is the summit seen from the Simplon side. Further round on the main ridge is pt. 3866m. marking the top of the SE ridge of the mtn. First ascent: M. Amherdt with J. Zumkemmi and F. Klausen, 28 August, 1854. In winter: A. & R. Calegari and G. Scotti, 1 January, 1914. On ski: A. von Martin with O. Supersaxo, 22 March 1918.

North-West Ridge. Most ascents of the mtn. are made by this route from the Weissmies hut. The route is fairly direct, interesting, and is invariably taken as the first stage for making a traverse over the mtn. to the Lagginhorn. PD. First ascent: Probably J. D. James with Ambros Supersaxo, July, 1889.

10. From the Weissmies hut a cairned path crosses stony ground to the E. Take this for a few min., then follow a branch to the N which approaches the foot of the WSW ridge of the Lagginhorn. Keep L along the lateral moraine of the Tälli

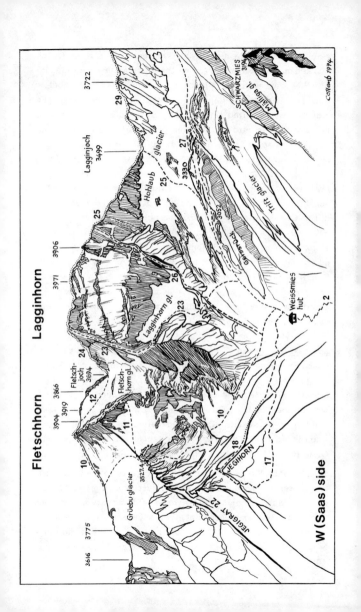

Fletschhorn **Lagginhorn**

3616 3775

Gruebu glacier

3904 3919 3866 3971 3906 25 29 3722

12 Fletsch-joch 3694

24 23

Fletschhorn gl.

11 3527.4

10 Lagginhorn gl. 23

26

25 Hohlaub glacier Lagginjoch 3499

27

3330

3052

Grasserjoch Triff glacier

23

Weissmies hut

10

2

18 JEGIHORN

17

JEGIGRAT 22

W (Saas) side

SCHWARZMIES 3104

Mellige gl.

Cottenb 1974

glacier, to where the moraine runs out on to the glacier (track marked on map, 30 min.). Cross the dry glacier on a diagonal line NNE and reach the opposite side at a circular hollow below a long scree and snow slope rising in the same direction to the ridge above. Climb this slope with a good zigzag track and reach the ridge midway between pts. 3451m. and 3527.4m. (track on map, 1½ h.). The ridge gives pleasant scrambling on sound scratched rocks. Pass just below pt. 3527.4m. and so reach the last rocks in the neck under the snowy western shoulder of the mtn. (30 min.). Climb the snow shoulder for about 200m., then slant L (NE) across the upper snowfield of the Gruben glacier, making a rising traverse to reach to NW ridge at a shoulder (c.3810m.) which is some distance along the ridge from pt. 3775m. This rising traverse steepens as one nears the ridge and one or two bergschrunds are crossed (1 h.). Now climb the NW ridge, snow, with cornices possible on the L in the upper part. At the top cross a crevassed snowfield and reach the summit rocks from the R (30 min., about 4 h. from Weissmies hut. 2 h. in descent).

South-West (Topham) Ridge. The great whaleback ridge of sound rock descending behind the Lagginhorn towards the Weissmies hut. Few ascents are made by this route, which is quite direct but more time consuming than the normal way. PD with pitches of II. The lower part of the ridge is now loose and tricky because of glacier recession. A convenient variation is described below. First ascent: H.W. Topham and G.H. Rendall with Aloys Supersaxo, 16 July, 1887.

11. From the Weissmies hut follow Route 10 to the foot of the snowy western shoulder of the mtn. just beyond pt. 3527.4m. (2½ h.). Make an horizontal traverse R (SE) across snow slopes to a short steep snow/ice inlet giving access to the ridge which is reached below pt. 3717m. (30 min.). Now follow the ridge as directly as possible with a number of small pitches some

of which are easily taken on the R side. At the top of this section traverse directly over the hoof-like gendarme pt. 3914m. to a small gap. Continue with similar climbing and interest to a snow crest and the summit (2-2½ h., about 5½ h. from Weissmies hut).

From Fletschjoch. This col, called Fletschhornjoch on LK25 (3694m.), lies between the Fletschhorn and Lagginhorn. Looking at the Fletschhorn there is a snow cwm to the R of the summit and this provides the way up. In fact the route between the col and the summit is invariably used in descent, for traversing the mtn. to join the Lagginhorn. F.

12. From the summit descend E ridge on pleasant rocks then snow to a saddle (3904m.). From this descend slopes to the S into the snow cwm which is crossed to the col at the foot of the N ridge of the Lagginhorn (30 min. in descent, 45 min. in ascent).

South-East Ridge (Hohsassgrat). Hosaasgrat, LK25. Of the three ridges extending towards the Simplon road on the eastern side of the mtn., this is the steepest and most difficult. Compared with the other two it has sound rock and is effectively the normal route on this side. The Laggin bivouac is at its foot. The ridge is entirely rock, well defined in the first third, becoming progressively vaguer as it rises to the summit horseshoe at pt. 3866m. Snow on the rocks adds to the interest. Recommended. AD with short pitches of II/III. First ascent: F. Gardiner and T. Cox with Peter Knubel and J. Dorsaz, 5 July, 1876.

13. From the Laggin bivouac return along the hut approach path for two min., then take a track L up to the signal cairn 2791m. at the top of the moraine, small tarn. Ascend the terminal moraine and snow banks of the Zibelenfluh (Sibiluflue) glacier.

FLETSCHHORN E face

3104

13

3386

3539

3866 X

X 3919

3720

Sibilfluegat 14

Sibilflue glacier

Keep close to the side of the ridge and pass below pt. 3104m.
Climb the first slabby opening in the ridge after this pt., up
rocks and sometimes a snow ramp to a gap where the ridge
steepens. (The ridge can be reached at lower points, or in-
deed by starting directly up from the hut - longer). Climb the
broad crest, turning steep pitches on the L or R. Looser
grooves and small gullies can nearly always be used to avoid
frontal pitches which are however not really difficult. A saddle
point (3599m.) is reached. From just below this make a convenient traverse L into a big couloir, cross it (snow, delicate)
and climb the other side up to the enclosing parallel ridge.
Follow this as directly as possible, a narrow crest of good
rock with several nice pitches, and exit at pt. 3866m. (4-
$4\frac{1}{2}$ h.). Continue round the snowy horseshoe over pt. 3919m.
to the main summit (another 20 min.).

14. East Ridge (Zibelenfluhgrat). Sibilufluegrat, LK25. A
long rock ridge preceded by secondary summits of the Rothorn
before it rises into the summit mass. The rock is generally
poor. From the Laggin bivouac it is possible to avoid the
lower part by climbing to the ridge up a couloir from the Zibelenfluh glacier (approached as for Route 13), which is reached
in a gap above pt. 3235m. Rarely climbed. PD. 5 h. to summit. First ascent, to head of ridge just short of pt. 3919m.:
G. F. and G. B. Gugliermina, P. Schiavi and G. Caron, 20
July, 1900.

15. North-East Ridge (Breitlaubgrat). Breitloibgrat, LK25.
The long ridge descending towards Simplon village. Many
years ago it had a following but is now almost completely abandoned. Pleasant mixed climbing with easy but loose rocks.
The ridge is reached at pt. 3331.9m. by a long traverse from
the upper part of Route 8, across the Griessernen and Rossboden glacier plateau. PD-. About 9 h. from Simplon village.

First ascensionists.

<u>North (Rossboden) Face</u>. This splendid wall of 750m. is contained from L to R between the NE and NW ridges. At rather more than half-height a large rock band extends more than halfway across the face and is capped by séracs and ice walls. Beyond this, under the NW ridge, there is a broad opening of snow and ice before the face is closed again on the far R side by a series of rock ribs. The original (Blanchet) route penetrated the main rock barrier near the centre of the face then slanted steeply L under the séracs before returning R to join the NE ridge near the summit. This route is very dangerous, being raked by constant stonefall and falling ice. Not recommended. TD. E.R. Blanchet with O. Supersaxo and K. Mooser, 25 July, 1928, in $5\frac{1}{2}$ h. It has been repeated once, in 1948.

On the occasion of the third ascent of the face a new and much safer line was followed. This is the Viennese Route. It takes the snow/ice opening to the R of the summit line. This route is recommended and in ideal conditions has minimal exposure to falling rocks and ice. The climbing is entirely on snow/ice with long sections of 40-50° and steeper crux pitches. TD. E. Eidher, G. Godai, K. Mach, P. Pernitsch, H. Regele, E. Vanis and W. Wehrle, 17 July, 1960. First British ascent: R.J. Collister and R.I. Ferguson, 5 August, 1970.

A convenient and comfortable bivouac can be made on the small saddle pt. 3014m. in the rib dividing the Griessernen and Rossboden glaciers. Snow melt available nearby.

16. From Simplon village follow Route 8 for the Rossbodenpass as far as the lower end of the Griessernen glacier (2650m.). Now make tracks to the S, climbing snow slopes towards the top L corner of the glacier. Near the top move L on to the enclosing rib which is crossed in a few min. by a slight descent to the upper snowfield of the Rossboden glacier. Pt. 3014m.,

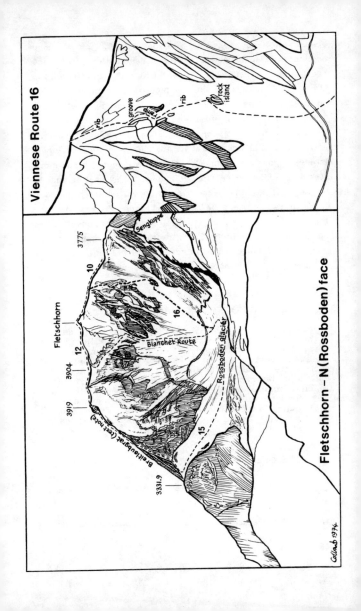

Viennese Route 16

rib
groove
dièdre
rib
rock island

Fletschhorn – N (Rossboden) face

3775
Sengkuppe
10
Fletschhorn
12
3904
39l9
Bretttermgrat (text note)
3331.9
15
Rossboden glacier
16
Blanchet Route

Callas.b 1974

bivouac site (about 4 h. from Simplon village). Cross a huge badly crevassed terrace in the Rossboden glacier to the S and reach more level slopes leading to the foot of the face (45 min.). Start in the centre below the conspicuous ice corridor leading up the R-hand part of the face, which at one third height has a rock island at the R side.

Cross the main bergschrund, possibly others, and go up directly and normally on snow at 40° for 250m. to the rock island (stonefall possible from R). Continue trending L and more steeply on a snow/ice rib (50°), past a tiny rock island, to below the R end of the sérac barrier above. A steep ice pitch leads to its foot where the barrier is breached by a ramp slant - ing R. Climb this for 25m. (60-70°) to an easier groove leading on to a rib in two pitches. Follow the rib, steepening to the corniced NW ridge which is reached about 15 min. from the summit (7-9 h. for face).

JÄGIHORN (JEGIHORN) 3206.3m.

A rock peak marking the SW end of the splendid gneiss ridge of the Jägigrat, which in turn is an extension of the Fletschhorn. The whole ridge is seen to advantage from the Weissmies hut. Some of the best rock climbs of the training variety at Saas are found on the ridge. The SE flank of the ridge, called the Jägiwand, is a network of routes and variations of which the main ones are given below. The advent of the cableway from the valley has reduced this rock playground to a day's outing in the way that the Aig. de l'M, Peigne and Pélerins are treated from cableways at Chamonix. Parties have no need to stay overnight at the hut.

Jägihorn routes

South-West Flank. The easiest route, a useful training walk. F.

17. From the Weissmies hut a small track makes a descending

traverse N, then turns W across the streams flowing between moraines below the Tälli glacier. The track vanishes in moraine; continue the traverse round below a landslide pile below the foot of the S rib of the Jägihorn. Traces of a path appear in grassy slopes leading up and round to the W (c. 2600m.), which form the SW side of the mtn. The slopes are named Weng on LK25. Leave the path at c. 2700m. and climb more or less direct over stony ground to reach the W ridge at c. 3050m. Follow the ridge to the summit ($2\frac{1}{4}$ h. from hut).

<u>South-East Couloir.</u> More direct than the previous route. This scree gully lies to the L(W) of the S rib of the mtn. and R of the larger southern shoulder, and gives a steep scramble. The couloir exits on the W ridge about 50m. from the summit. F. The normal route for most parties.

18. From the Weissmies hut approach as for Route 17. Do not go round the apparent foot of the S rib as indicated on map. Instead, climb directly up scree on E side of mtn., keeping L, then traverse L round the foot of the S rib proper, which starts a long way up from its apparent foot (track for this section shown on map). On the L(W) side of the rib is the couloir leading to the W ridge and the summit. There are traces of a path all the way ($1\frac{1}{2}$ h. from hut).

<u>South Rib.</u> A fine short rock climb, recommended. By easiest way, III, with more direct optional pitches of IV/V. 200m. First ascent: E. R. Blanchet, solo, 19 September, 1922.

19. Start as for Route 17, then 18, and reach the foot of the rib near where the couloir of Route 18 is entered (30 min.). The rib starts with an impressive tower about 50m. high. The direct ascent of this is V. Most parties avoid it by climbing up the couloir on the L to where a ledge can be taken R, to reach the rib above the lower major difficulty. Climb a pitch on the crest to below a large gendarme, overhanging on the L. Take an obvious chimney slanting L below the overhang and rejoin the crest higher up (III+). Follow the rib to a dislocation in its direction. Move R into a line of chimneys which lead up parallel to the rib to the top (III). Alternatively, after the first chimney move L and rejoin the rib (IV), and climb it by a series of fine, exposed slabs (IV+) ($1\frac{1}{2}$-$2\frac{1}{2}$ h. from hut).

20. South-East Face. On the R of the S rib, facing the hut, this steep wall has a number of routes and variations. The easiest are III, the hardest V. The height is about 250m. The most obvious line is formed by chimneys which are reached from the L by ledges and a slanting couloir with one difficult pitch; the start of these ledges is above the lowest point of the face and about 35m. below the foot of the S rib. The chimney line goes up just R of a conspicuous yellow patch on the face. First ascent: E. R. Blanchet with Josef Imseng, 4 September, 1918.

North-East Ridge. This short ridge comes down to the gap 3098m. which separates the Jägihorn from the Jägigrat. The approach is up a narrow couloir (Couloir Puiseux) well shown on map. II+ on ridge. Descended by P. Puiseux and party, 6 August, 1900.

21. Approach as for Route 17 and from the moraine bed of the Tälli cwm climb straight up a scree funnel into the couloir below the gap. The couloir is steep, narrow and somewhat unpleasant in the upper part, but not difficult. From the gap climb the sharp, steep crest of the ridge to the summit ($1\frac{1}{2}$ h. from Weissmies hut).

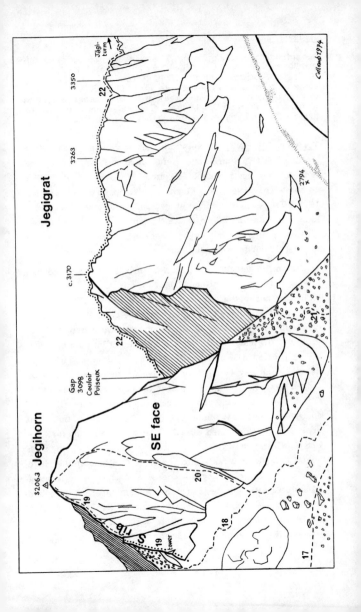

<u>Jägigrat</u> 3350m. 3368m. 3451m.

See introduction to Jägihorn. The ridge proper starts at the gap 3098m. at the foot of the short NE ridge of the Jägihorn (Route 21). From here the first section over a rocky knoll along to pt. 3350m. is covered by large blocks. After that it is very narrow and crenellated, with the notable Jägiturm (3368m.) and Grand Gendarme. The ridge ends at a small tower (3451m.) near a junction with a spur running NW.

<u>Traverse SW - NE.</u> A very popular traverse on excellent rock. III/III+. Spare rope useful for abseiling. A traverse in the other direction involves a pitch of V (rarely done). First complete traverse: W. Bloch with T. Bumann, 14 August, 1917. To reach the ridge at gap 3098m. the shortest route is up the Puiseux couloir (Route 21, 1 h. from hut). However it is more pleasant but longer to ascend by Route 18 and descend the NE ridge of the Jägihorn to the gap (about 2 h.).

22. From the gap 3098m. follow the broad ridge over rocks, stones and some snow to pt. 3350m. (30 min.).

The next part of the ridge is steep and narrow. Either climb down it (III+) or make two abseils into the gap below. Above, climb straight up the Jägiturm (3368m.) without particular difficulty (II) and from its top make an abseil into the next gap before the Grand Gendarme (III by climbing down). (This gendarme which has two points can be avoided fairly easily by ledges on the L, but this escapes the point of the traverse). Climb the sharp and exposed crest to the first point (II+) and continue delicately to the second (III). Now descend the steep crest for 10-15m. then abseil about 15m. to a comfortable ledge. Climb down the next section to just above a gap, then abseil 8m. down a wall into the gap. Continue up the ridge near the crest, climbing a succession of sustained pitches of III and III+ with belay pegs in place. A large block on the ridge can be crossed (IV+) or turned on the R. Finish in a gap to the SW of pt. 3451m. (4-5 h. from pt. 3350m.).

Descend by an easy couloir in the SE flank of the ridge to

to join the track of Route 10 above the Tälli glacier (1 h. , about 8 h. for round trip).

Note: There are several direct routes up the SE wall (Jägi-wand) of the Jägigrat, to reach the crest near the Jägiturm, so avoiding the easy part of the ridge. III+/IV.

FLETSCHJOCH 3694m.

Fletschhornjoch on LK25. Between the Fletschhorn and Lag-ginhorn. Not of much value as a pass and rarely crossed. W(Weissmies hut) side, AD. E (Laggin biv. side), D. See also Route 12. First traverse: F. W. Jacomb and G. Chater with C. Michel and P. Baumann, 15 August, 1863.

LAGGINHORN 4010.1m.

A striking mtn. , standing conspicuously above the Weissmies hut, and formed like a gable roof top. The rock is gneiss, fairly good, and gives routes of general mountaineering inter-est. A popular ascent either for itself or as a traverse with the Fletschhorn. The latter is easily the most attractive ex-pedition. The mtn. is often climbed by solo alpinists because crevassed slopes can be avoided. There is no satisfactory direct route on the E side of the mtn. The huge E spur can be taken from the Laggin biv. , but it is loose, complicated, sub-ject to stonefall and not recommended. AD.

First ascent: E. L. Ames, 3 others and J. J. Imseng with F. Andenmatten and 3 other guides, 26 August, 1856. In winter and on ski: H. Rey and L. Gelpke with H. Supersaxo, 22 March 1918.

West-South-West Ridge. The ordinary route, in good condi-tions entirely rock, although the upper section is normally mixed with snow and possibly ice in narrow gutters between rock ribs. Somewhat monotonous climbing. In good conditions the ridge is quite safe for solo climbers. PD. First ascen-sionists.

23. From the Weissmies hut a cairned path crosses stony ground to the E. In a few min. it bears N but a branch con-tinues E. Take the R branch to the E which approaches the

lower end of the Hohlaub glacier. Do not go up too far; find a secondary line of cairns to the N, over very rough ground, and cross the foot of the WSW subsidiary ridge coming down from the S ridge of the mtn. (Alternatively, this point can be reached by staying on the path running N, for a few min., till a fork at pt. 2809m. is reached. Here go up a track E on a moraine crest to the same point). This leads to the small Lagginhorn glacier which lies between the main WSW ridge and the aforesaid subsidiary WSW ridge of the mtn. Climb up this glacier, rarely crevassed and usually hard snow, and turn a rock buttress projecting from the main ridge below pt. 3355m. Immediately behind this projection get on to the rocks and climb them to the crest (large boulders, ledges and short walls, steepening towards the top) at a fairly level place indicated as pt. 3539m. on map. (Alternatively, cross the foot of the small Lagginhorn glacier at c. 3000m. and reached the foot of the WSW ridge proper. Climb this tediously, traces of a path, over pt. 3355m. to the level place mentioned above). ($2\frac{1}{4}$ h.).

Continue along the broad ridge over large blocks to where it steepens and goes straight up to the summit. The rocks are generally snowy, on a sort of facet, and this can be avoided in poor conditions by climbing steeper rock on its R edge, more friable but not difficult. Climb directly to the summit ($1\frac{3}{4}$ h., 4 h. from Weissmies hut. 2 h. in descent). This route has the advantage of being free from crevassed slopes.

North-North-East Ridge. A narrow, delicate ridge rising from the Fletschjoch, invariably climbed as a stage in traversing the Fletschhorn and Lagginhorn. See Route 12. Alternate rock and snow crests, sometimes heavily corniced. Interesting with no real technical difficulty. PD+. First ascent: W. A. B. Coolidge with Chr. and R. Almer; and G. Broke with A. and T. Andenmatten, 27 July, 1887.

24. From the Fletschjoch follow the crest of the steep ridge as closely as possible. There is a small shoulder halfway up, where if cornices are formed a delicate traverse to the R may be necessary ($1\frac{1}{2}$ - 2 h.).

<u>South Ridge</u>. Starts from the Lagginjoch (3499m.-). This is the longest ridge of the mtn. and rather more technical than the others. It is entirely rock, but with snow crests along the roof-like section beyond the big gendarme (3906m.). PD+. Quite interesting, some of the rock is loose. First ascent: W. E. Utterson-Kelso and two ladies, with P. Knubel, J. M. Blumenthal and J. P. Zurbrücken, 11 August, 1883.

25. From the Weissmies hut a cairned path crosses stony ground to the E. In a few min. a branch bears L(N); ignore this. Continue E over grassy rocks then moraine to the true L bank of the Hohlaub glacier at a place a short distance NE of pt. 3052m. Climb up the S side of the glacier, pass to the L of rock island pt. 3330m. (or to the R if there are bad crevasses), then turn NE across snow to reach the Lagginjoch by a short scree slope (2 h.).

From the col the crest is followed exactly except at a step which is turned on the L. Pass the junction with the WSW subsidiary ridge and reach the large gendarme (3906m.). This can be traversed or turned on the L ($2\frac{1}{2}$ h.). Cross a snow gap and continue up the crest to a broad knoll (3971m.), which is crossed without difficulty. The ridge narrows again and leads to a sharp gendarme preceding a gap. Turn the former on the R, and from the gap climb on the crest to the summit (1 h., $3\frac{1}{2}$ h. from Lagginjoch, $5\frac{1}{2}$ h. from Weissmies hut).

26. <u>West-South-West Subsidiary Ridge</u>. This ridge has some interest as a major variation to Route 25, inasmuch as it avoids any crevassed glacier. The route joins the S ridge about

150m. S of the big gendarme (3906m.). PD+. Climb the ridge from its base (Route 23). At mid-height it is narrow with slabs and cracks of some difficulty; these pitches can be avoided by ledges down to the L. The ridge is rejoined as soon as possible and followed to the junction with the S ridge (4 h. to junction from hut).

LAGGINJOCH 3499m.

The pass between the Lagginhorn and Weissmies. Rarely crossed but used to reach the main ridges of both mtns. from one side or the other. Saas side, F, 2 h. from Weissmies hut. Laggin side, AD, about 6 h. from Laggin hut. See Routes 25 and 29 respectively. First recorded traverse: J. Robertson and C. G. Heathcote with F. Andenmatten, P. Venetz and P. Zurbrücken, 1 August, 1864.

WEISSMIES 4023m.

The principal peak of this chain; it has a moderate outline and the normal routes are easy snow climbs. The ridges are more interesting, and one is classic. The best outing for the average climber is to traverse the mtn. to the Zwischbergen-pass and return via Almagelleralp to Saas. It has an impressive E face, commanding the Laggintal, and this provides some difficult mixed climbing. The ordinary route is easily the most popular climb in the chain, and the mtn. is one of the easiest 4000 m. peaks in the Alps.

First ascent: J.K. Heusser and P.J. Zurbriggen, August, 1855. In winter: A. von Martin and H. Rumpelt, 25 March, 1910. On Ski: A. Bonacossa and G.F. Casati Brioshi, 12 April, 1924.

<u>Trift Glacier and South-West Ridge (Triftgrat)</u>. Not the easiest route up the mtn., but the normal one when starting from the Weissmies hut, and the route by which most ascents are made. Entirely on snow and glacier terrain, steep in places, interesting. F+. There is usually a good trail in summer. The variants from the lower part of the Trift glacier, reached by a horizontal track still in good condition from the hut, are longer, more difficult and, above all, complicated by the state of the glacier.

27. From the Weissmies hut take a small cairned track to the E over grassy rocks then moraine to the true L bank of the Hohlaub glacier at a place a short distance NE of pt. 3052m. Climb up this S side of the glacier, parallel with the flattish rock spur of the Geissrück further S, then cross the head of the rock spur by passing to the R(S) of the rock islet pt. 3330m. From the last rocks cross an intermediate glacier plateau horizontally to the SSE and skirt close to the rock toe, pt. 3271m. LK50 (2 h.). Here, a lower pt. 3210m. is now indicated on LK25.

In practice some guides take a slightly lower, cairned route across the Geissrück, arriving at the R bank of the Trift glacier where the rocks disappear in the ice, immediately below and W of pt. 3271m. There are several crevasses here and the

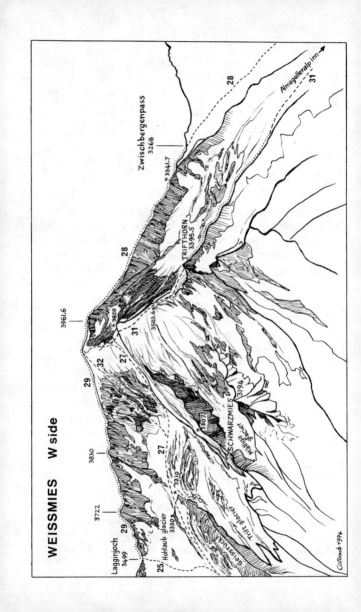

WEISSMIES   W side

Lagginjoch
3499

3722

3830

3961.6

28

28

Zwischbergenpass
3269

× 3341.7

TRIFTHORN
3395.5

Almagelleralp imm

31

31

3620

3503.6

29

32

27

31

27

SCHWARZMIES
3194

3397

27

3210

25

Hohlaub glacier
3303

29

Geisruck

Trift glacier

Triftrucke

Mätthe
glacier

Collomb 1974

glacier is climbed to the central plateau in a few min. (this approach is 15-20 min. shorter).

Cross the plateau to the S and reach the foot of a big snow/ice slope. Cross the bergschrund (c. 3400m.), sometimes quite wide, and climb directly towards pt. 3820 above. The slope is 45° and is sometimes cut by simple crevasses. At 3700m. it eases off. Trend L under pt. 3820m. and reach the ridge at a saddle nearer the summit; cornice ($1\frac{1}{2}$ h.). Keep L along the broad ridge, cross a bergschrund and slant L then R up the last easy but steeper slope to the top (30 min., 4 h. from hut).

South-South-East Ridge. This is the easiest way up the mtn., but it is rarely used for ascent. The ridge is usually descended to make a traverse. The ridge starts at the Zwischbergenpass (3268m.); this point is slightly above and to the NW of the lowest point (3242m.), between the Weissmies and Portjenhorn. In descent the route is extremely quick because one can benefit from long glissades. F.

28. From the Almagelleralp inn climb a short track to the foot-path above and N of the inn. Follow this, crossing an old cableway terminus platform, to a stream shored up with con-crete banks (2449m.). Cross it and in a few steps reach a fork. Take the secondary L branch in steep zigzags with old paint flashes up the Giw pastures, and enter the cwm alongside the Weisstal (Wysstal) stream (2783m.). The path passes below the S side of Dri Horlini and eventually disappears. Climb directly towards the L-hand of the two cols of the Zwisch-bergenpass and reach it by scree and a scramble over rocks ($2\frac{1}{2}$h., $1\frac{1}{2}$h. in descent).

From the pass traverse across the R flank of the ridge below the schist knoll pt. 3341.7 m. Scree and snow lead to the long snow slope lying on the E side of the ridge, which narrows at the top. Climb straight up the slope to its head (c. 3800m.). The rocks above it are easy and there are traces of a path. The rocks form a triangle which leans back and narrows to a ridge

capped by pt. 3961.6m. (15 min. for this section). A few more rocks lead to the snowy summit ridge which is sometimes corniced on the R (in which case drop down a little to the L). In normal conditions it takes 15 min. to cross it and reach the summit ($2\frac{1}{2}$h. on average from the pass, 5h. from Almagelleralp inn; in descent, 45 min. to the pass with glissading, $2\frac{1}{4}$h. all told to the inn).

North Ridge. The classic route and one of the best climbs of its class in the Saas region. The ridge starts at the Lagginjoch and is quite long; the first two-thirds are rock of average quality, the last part is snow. The ridge is prone to verglas which affects the difficulty to a marked degree. Normally AD, with numerous short pitches of III and one of IV. The snow section is fairly easy. Reaching the Lagginjoch from the Laggin hut has been done perhaps only 10 times in the last 12 years. This latter approach is more worrying than the ridge itself. AD. First ascent: W.H. Paine and Miss E. Paine with T. Andenmatten and another man, 25 August, 1884.

29. From the Weissmies hut reach the Lagginjoch by Route 25 (2h.). From the Laggin bivouac descend the steeply scarped grass slope to the S and reach a fixed cable at the edge of a steeper drop. Go down this into a couloir and continue down to exit R at the bottom. By traversing, go up on to the L lateral moraine of the Holutrift glacier, cross the rubble-covered ice below a badly crevassed section and climb on to the opposite moraine. The loss of height is 200m. Go up the moraine to its head, then slant L across a shallow moraine and snow hollow, rising all the time to the rocks immediately below the E spur of the Lagginhorn. A tiny step forming the absolute base of this spur, some way below, is pt. 2776m. Climb a short but conspicuous gully-gangway up the supporting rocks to a gap on the front of the spur, with a large tower immediately below ($2\frac{1}{4}$h.). Continue at this level along ledges and terraces, working up and down and crossing frequent couloirs all in broken rock and partly snow covered but generally easy, right across the lower part of the Lagginhorn SE face, till at the far side a fairly obvious and slightly rising snowy ledge line leads onto the N ridge of the mtn. about 150m. away from the Lagginjoch, which is soon reached by a short descent. Allow 3-4h. to traverse the face. Except after a fine cold night, stonefall danger on the face is considerable. AD.

From the Lagginjoch climb straight up the edge of a long series of slabs (II+) which overhang the E side. Half-way up to pt. 3722m. reach the grande dalle. This steep face is climbed direct on the R(W) side. Start up on small rounded holds, then direct aid from fixed pegs in turn is taken to overcome the pitch. It is possible to lassoo the first peg; finish on somewhat doubtful rock which is quite steep (25m., IV then III). The ridge eases off and leads easily to pt. 3722m. (1¾h.). Much of the rock in this first section is somewhat loose.

The next section is very narrow and cut by gaps and small gendarmes. The best course is to stay on the crest and traverse them (delicate, bits of III). The rock is worse on the flanks. One gendarme overhangs noticeably and this can be turned on the L. Abseiling on this section is pointless. Finally approach pt. 3830m. where snow crests may be found. Climb over this large knoll (1½h.), and descend a little before going up the last rocks to the upper snow arête (30 min.). The arête is climbed keeping slightly R of the crest (cornices on L) and it leads easily to the summit (30 min., about 4¼h. from col, 6¼h. from Weissmies hut, 10-11h. from Laggin bivouac).

North-East Flank and North Ridge. This is the best, easiest and safest route from the Laggin Bivouac. Mixed climbing, interesting, PD+. The way up to the N ridge is by the spur immediately to the S of a less prominent one rising to pt. 3830m. on the N ridge. Descended by P. Escher with T. Biner and

A. Andenmatten, 16 August 1919.

30. From the Laggin bivouac descend as for the N ridge above, and from the S-side moraine of the Holutrift glacier continue up until it is convenient to traverse S and reach the foot of the Lagginhorn E spur, with pt. 2776 on the first little step above (2h.). Continue over moraine/scree then on to the Laggin glacier, normally badly crevassed but not steep. Work up its centre, almost due S, keeping mid-way between the Lagginhorn face and the broken lower edge of the glacier. Keep bearing slightly L(SE), traversing the breadth of the glacier to reach a broad snow spur rising off the S side, towards the N ridge. Get on to this from the L (falling ice on R), with pt. 3028m. further L, and climb the snow slope to its highest L-hand corner. Now join rocks of a steep, well-marked ridge, normally carrying a fair amount of snow. Follow this to a junction with the N ridge, which is reached at the last easy rock section before the final snow arête. Continue along the ridge to the top ($3\frac{1}{2}$h., $5\frac{1}{2}$h. from Laggin bivouac).

South-West Side. Several approaches can be made from Almagelleralp to the SW ridge (Triftgrat). All of them involve hard going on trackless stony terrain, c.f. the Steintälli cwm. The most comfortable and acceptable "line" is an unrecorded one of virtually no difficulty, up the Rottal cwm under the S face of the mtn. PD-.

31. From the Almagelleralp inn climb a short track to the foot-path above and N of the inn. Follow this, crossing an old cableway terminus platform, to a stream shored up with concrete banks (2449m.). Cross it and in a few steps reach a fork. Take the secondary L branch in steep zigzags on grass. After 10 min. this track (Zwischbergenpass) trends R. Leave it and climb directly towards the Rottal cwm above (NE). In doubt, do not go higher up the Zwischbergen track than the top of a pavement-like section ending at ruined stone-wall huts among

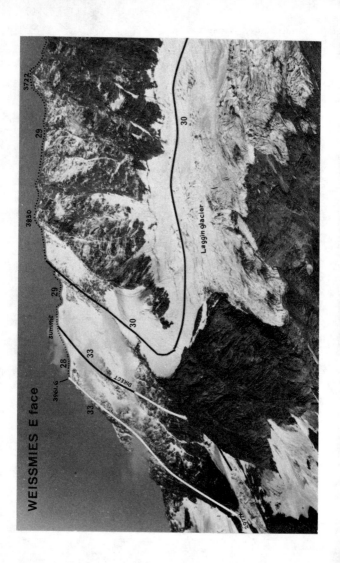

Lagginjoch.

Heinhrite glacier

Laggin glacier

30

III + route
3074 to col

29

29

29

25.

3499

3722

3930

29

2776

rocks. A vague track goes some distance towards the cwm, over steep rough ground. Aim to keep R of an old moraine lake (2973m.) and cross the cwm bed to pt. 3067m. Now make a flanking movement L(WNW) over a low moraine ridge, then steep scree, and under the rocks of pt. 3820m. on the main ridge above. Continue between the foot of these rocks and a lower rock barrier so that moraine then snow is reached on the SW facet of pt. 3820m. Climb this snow slope, L-wards into narrows, then towards the centre, and finish at its highest point. A short rock barrier, loose and generally snowy, is climbed to the upper snow slope leading to the snow dome of pt. 3820m. A more pleasant alternative, cornice permitting, is to move L below the barrier and take a few steep rocks on to the main snow arête below and L of the snow dome ($5\frac{1}{2}$h.). Soon after crossing pt. 3820 the ridge is joined by the usual route from the Weissmies hut (another hour).

32. <u>West Face Direct.</u> Immediately L of the bergschrund and big slope taken by the ordinary Triftgrat route (27) is a rock and ice wall some 400m. high, extending L into this flank of the N ridge. It is surmounted by a sérac barrier then easier summit slopes. Three distinct rock masses mark this wall. The first on the R, nearest the ordinary route, has been climbed up its L side by an ice slope of 50-55°, followed by rock pitches of III to below the séracs. An exit R up the barrier involves ice climbing at 70°. TD. First ascent: E. Vanis and Ruth Steinmann, 29 July, 1971.

33. <u>East Face.</u> This is a fine-looking and remote wall about 1000m. high. To climb it from the Laggin biv. involves descending 300m. before the approach is begun. There is no hut or convenient chalet in the deep Laggintal below the face. The face is formed by a huge shallow depression contained between the spur of Route 30 and a parallel NE spur descending from pt. 3961.6m. on the SE ridge. The latter spur (base pt. 2977m.) was climbed by E. Allegra with A. Dorsaz, 24 August, 1901. The route adheres to the crest with some difficulty at first. When it eases a traverse R is made to cross a couloir and join a parallel but vaguer mixed rib, quite easy. In turn this leads to snow/ice slopes which are climbed to the main ridge between pt. 3961.6m. and the summit. Serious stonefall danger. 1000m. AD/D. The upper part of the main spur was descended by G. W. and Mrs. Murray with O. and A. Supersaxo, 27 August, 1931. This is much safer and better climbing (i. e. all the way on the main spur) and is recommended. AD. About 7 h. from Laggin biv. to summit. For the approach, descend to pt. 2474m. on moraine below the Weissmies glacier, then ascend this moraine and snow to the foot of the spur, pt. 2977m.

The original route on the face went up its moderately inclined R-hand side, close to the spur of Route 30. The exact line is not known but the rock is broken and this part of the face is raked by stonefall. E. P. and Mrs. Jackson and J. A. Peebles with P. Schlegel, U. Rubi and J. Martin, 17 August, 1876.

A direct line in the middle of the face, using most of the snow/ice slopes available, was made by J. Braun, B. Meyer, M. Brandt, G. Paratte and R. Theytaz, up and down, 19 July, 1967, in 8 h. from hut to summit. 1000m. AD. From the approach to the route on the spur to the L (see above), reach the centre of the face at c. 3100m. Climb on to the minor spur on the immediate L of the main drainage channel from the hanging glacier in the upper part of the face (some stonefall, etc.). Moderately difficult rocks on the spur lead to a snow section and a continuation spur follows. This exits on to the hanging glacier which is climbed (50°) to finish just L of the summit.

SCHWARZMIES 3194m.

This peaklet of crystalline gneiss forms a ridge of gendarmes at the end of a secondary spur detached WNW from the SW ridge of the Weissmies. It is situated directly above and SE of the Grund cableway terminus, from which an approach can be made in 2h. The normal route is from the highest conspicuous gap in the W ridge, reached from the S side (II+). The lower part of this ridge gives a longer and better rock climb, with abseils off the gendarmes leading into the upper gap (III+). A descent can be made along the jagged E ridge, essentially horizontal, as the descent gap at the far end is slightly higher than the summit tower. Turning movements, abseils, reascents of gendarmes and various steps are involved (III/III+). Allow 3h. for complete traverse.

DRI HORLINI 3096m. 3210m.

A very popular practice rock climb, from the Almagelleralp inn. It is a red rock rib rising in three step-like summits, the lowest of which is pt. 3096. The S side of the rib is a long rock wall about 150m. high. This side overlooks the track leading to the Zwischbergenpass.

Complete Traverse. An excellent training climb on perfect rock, III/IV. First traverse: G. E. Kruseman and O. Supersaxo and A. Bumann, 5 July, 1929.

34. From the Almagelleralp inn follow Route 28 to where the track crosses R over the stream as you leave the grass and enter the rocky Wysstal cwm. Climb L(NW) over scree and large blocks to a large grassy patch making a conspicuous indentation at the foot of the rock wall below and L(SW) of pt. 3096. Start up a grassy gangway slanting R, then climb a steep crack (10m., III) leading into a couloir. Follow this to a small gap at the top. The imposing step above is climbed by a crack trending R to an overhang, and this is overcome by moving L to reach the main ridge (IV). Alternatively, turn the step easily on the L and climb to the ridge. Follow the mossy crest and turn a large block on the L or R before reaching the first summit (3096m.). Continue along the crest with short pitches to

28

DRI HORLINI Route 34.

the second top, after which a level section cut by small gaps leads to a smooth slab. Take this direct (IV) and continue to the summit of a gendarme. Descend by a vertical abseil and so reach the third top and a higher summit of scree (3210m.).

To return, continue along the main ridge on scree until it is convenient to descend into the cwm immediately below the Zwischbergenpass, where Route 28 is rejoined. Allow 3h. for the traverse and the same time again for the approach and descent.

TÄLLIHORN 3448m.

The first summit on the ridge winding eastwards from the Weissmies, from which it is separated by the broad Weiss-miessattel (3406m.). The summit is a characteristic rock-head, extended by a ridge in the direction of the saddle, to a forepeak (3442.2m.). The mtn. is seldom climbed. A direct route from Almagelleralp inn crosses the Zwischbergenpass, and without losing height traverses below the Weissmiessattel to the snowfield on the S flank of the summit, which is then easily reached ($3\frac{1}{2}$ h. from inn). The N ridge gives a fine rock climb (III+, G.I. Finch and F. Schjelderup, 2 August, 1913) which can be done from the Laggin biv., involving a descent of 300m. before the ridge can be approached.

First ascent, about 1850.

PART II

Portjengrat chain

Zwischbergenpass to Monte Moropass

ZWISCHBERGENPASS 3242m. 3268m.

Between the Weissmies and Portjenhorn (Portjengrat), from
the Almagelleralp inn to Gondo. An ancient pass across which
cattle have been driven. Frequented by walking and climbing
parties on the W side. The lowest point is blocked by a rock
wall on the E side, and a higher depression to the N (3268m.)
is used. F, both sides. For approach from W side see Route
28. See also previous entry on Tällihorn.

PORTJENGRAT

PIZZO D'ANDOLLA 3653.8m.

PORTJENHORN 3567m.

S of the Zwischbergenpass the main ridge of the chain, joined
by the political frontier between Switzerland and Italy at the
P. d'Andolla, its highest point, is noted for the quality of its
rock (crystalline gneiss). The first section, running approx.
N - S, ends at a gap called Portje (Port), at the S foot of the
Andolla. The continuation ridge is described under the head-
ings of Mittelrück and Sonniggrat.

Following the ridge from the Zwischbergenpass, the Portjenhorn summit is fairly insignificant, being the highest of a
series of ridge towers and gendarmes. This summit is rarely
visited (most routes, PD). After reaching a higher ridge pt.
3584m. beyond, the ridge drops a few m. before rising to the
P. d'Andolla proper. This is the Italian name for the summit
generally called Portjengrat on the Swiss side, although the
entire ridge purports to carry the same name.

The Portjenhorn was climbed in 1873. First ascent and traverse of P. d'Andolla or Portjengrat proper: C.T. Dent with
A. and F. Burgener, 7 September, 1871.

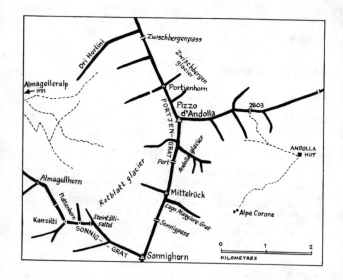

<u>Portjengrat (S-N. Traverse)</u>. One of the best rock climbs in the Saas district, reached directly from Almagelleralp, on perfect gneiss as rough as gabbro. The popularity of this route must account for the upkeep of the inn. Fresh snow clears quickly. PD in general with continuous climbing at II, several unavoidable pitches of III-/III and optional pitches possible though the best rock is always on the crest. The W subsidiary ridge variation for avoiding the first section starting at Portje is frequently used, though it is better, according to prevailing conditions, to use another variation between the subsidiary ridge and Portje (see below). The ridge in the reverse direction N-S (i.e. by the normal descent route) is rarely done and involves climbing the smooth N side summit slab (IV/IV+). First ascensionists, S-N.

35. From the Almagelleralp inn climb a short track to the footpath above and N of the inn. Follow this crossing an old cableway terminus platform, to a stream shored up with concrete banks (2449m.). Cross it and almost immediately pass a secondary fork rising up L (ignore, Zwischbergenpass). Continue by the main path which is joined at the stream crossing pt. 2561m. by a large track coming up from the valley below (original and now disused approach to Zwischbergenpass for men driving cattle). Continue the traverse line (a small path above leads to the Wysstal cwm), and on nearing the next stream the track goes directly up hill. After crossing the stream higher up the path is very faint, but good lines of cairns can be followed. Go up to and across a frontal moraine to the R and contour somewhat upwards and SE under the headland pt. 3007m. Reach a trench (slight descent) at the foot of roches moutonnées. Climb these along a dwindling spine till it is convenient to move R on to the snow slopes of the Rotblatt glacier, at c. 3050m. Ascend the slopes SSE (no crevasses) to reach a bergschrund and the gap of Portje (3295m.) on the R (3¼h.).

Above is a big initial step in the ridge, the ascent of which is the hardest part of the climb. From the gap traverse on to the L side of the ridge below the step and climb a series of nail-scratched slabs as directly as possible to the crest (III+). Follow the sharp crest, turning a rock finger on the L, and descend slightly to a small conspicuous saddle below the second step. This saddle is the point joined by the 1st. Variation (see below). Above, take a pleasant chimney line in the middle of the rock wall; after 25m. (III-) trend R and reach a ledge line working R, on to the Italian side of the step. Finish up steep rocks just behind the top of step (3492m.).

Continue along a sharp and barely rising crest. This has continuous little traverses up and down on the L side, at varying distances below the crest, but never more than 5-8m. On the L side, finally reach a steeper bit; get on to the crest by climbing steep broken rock (II+). Cross a little gap and climb the rock-head from where the W subsidiary ridge is detached (c. 3560m.). Junction with 2nd. Variation (1¾h.).

An almost level snow shoulder and a few rocks are now crossed to the foot of the summit ridge. Keep L then reach the broad crest at the far end. Climb a rock glacis, then go up a short gully under the L side of the first, largest and most serious gendarme on the ridge. The ways up this known to the author are as follows (there are others); (i) From the big flake gap at the top of the short gully traverse R and up to a stance. Climb the fine wall above, near the R edge, and trend L then R to the top of the gendarme (IV+). (ii) Pass L through the flake gap then move up a few m. On the R, and leading up steeply to the R, is a big conspicuous narrow slab, cut by a boot-width crack. Climb this, difficult to start (III+), then easily to a small shoulder. Move L and take a short wall to the top. This is the longest way in climbing distance. (iii) From the foot of the crack in (ii) continue straight up an obvious red corner, vertical to finish but with good hidden holds and peg runner in place for final pull up on to the rear/upper side of gendarme (IV). This is the shortest route, possibly icy in imperfect conditions.

Now either stay on the crest, or for convenience use traverse-type pitches just below it on the L side. Small steps and pinnacles follow in rapid succession, giving pleasant climbing at II and III. One gendarme can be taken through a hole. All the rock is heavily scratched. Finally reach on the crest a small gap below the summit head. From the L climb steeply then somewhat R, to the top of a crevassed rock. From the R step across the gap and pull up to the summit. Madonna and CAI Visitors' Book (1½h., about 6½h. from inn).

Descent: Go along ridge to the N, along an obvious easy line, to the top of a steep smooth slab. From comfortable ledges abseil 15m. down it from a wooden wedge jammed between two rocks, to a snow bank at the bottom. (In ascent this slab is climbable by a slight depression on the L side, looking up.

IV+. (A climbing route round the obstacle, alleged to be II+, could not be found by the guidebook survey party in 1971). Continue down a few snowy rocks to a narrow saddle in front of the first of four gendarmes which mark the short descent ridge. From the saddle descend a groove on the R side, vertical at first, but with good holds, and reach a boulder ledge at the bottom (II+). Traverse easily into the next gap before the 2nd gendarme. Now, do not take a tempting looking traverse line on the L side (IV). Turn it easily on the R, rising into the next gap. To complete the movement in avoiding the gendarme, now transfer to the L side, along a horizontal creviced ledge. Reach the head of a gully, with the 3rd gendarme on the L overhead. This gendarme can be traversed (probably III+), but the normal route seems to be as follows: avoid it by descending the gully for about 5m. (awkward snow in 1971); now either move L, facing out, into an open nail-scratched corner below the gap between gendarmes 3 and 4, and from a straddling position pull up into the gap; or descend a few m. further down the gully and attack the corner from below. Either way, awkward, III+. From the gap climb a crack for a few m. in the wall of the 4th gendarme, then reverse down another flake crack in a few m. to easy ledges. All difficulties end here. Go down snowy slabs and blocks on the crest till it is convenient to move L and join the snow slope coming up to the ridge just ahead, with pt. 3584m. further along (1h.).

Make a descending traverse L(NW) down the snow slope (in late season crossing alternate strips of loose scree) and reach a horizontal shoulder in the W ridge of the Portjenhorn, at c. 3300m. On the N side of this descend R then L to the bottom of another snow slope leading into a bouldery upper corner of the Wysstal cwm. Work R(N) down this, finally over low rocky terraces into the flat bed of the main cwm at 2960m., opposite Dri Horlini. Work across to the latter (N) side, join the Zwischbergen track and follow this down to junction with the approach route at stream crossing pt. 2449m. The upper part of this descent becomes unpleasant in late season, when the snow slopes dry out, leaving detestable rubble. F+ (2h., 3h. from summit to Almagelleralp inn).

<u>Variation I:</u> To avoid the first step in ridge above the Portje gap, join the first small saddle beyond it, well before the next step and junction with W subsidiary ridge (Var. II below). Go straight up the Rotblatt glacier to the obvious depression in rocks below the saddle. In mid season the loose lower terraced rocks are snow covered and reasonably firm; the upper depression is a steep snow band. Climb keeping slightly L at first, then in the centre, and finally up the R edge of the snow band. In late season, a bit unpleasant and delicate. PD. The saddle is at the foot of the chimney line in a wall (see above).

<u>Variation II:</u> W subsidiary ridge. This joins the main ridge at the intermediate snow shoulder, so avoiding all the lower part of the ridge. On the final moraine approach to the Rotblatt glacier, work more to the L, up rocky ground and either over or round (L side) the hillock of pt. 3007m. Continue due E on snow patches, passing the first and lowest step/tower of the W ridge, then climb R, on steep rubble or snow on to the ridge. Follow the winding ridge, with several isolated slabby pitches of II and III in the middle part. Difficulties are generally turned on the L side of crest. In the last section keep L of the apparent crest line and go up snow on to the large shoulder at the foot of the main summit ridge (about 45 min. shorter for complete ascent than complete ridge taken from the Portje gap).

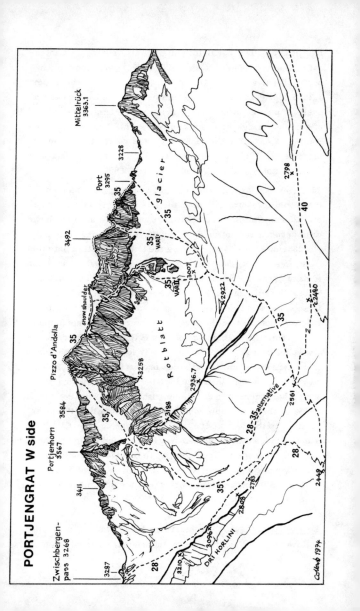

PORTJENGRAT W side

<u>East Ridge</u>. The usual Italian (Andolla) route, less inter-
esting than the classic traverse ridge. PD+ with short pitches
of III. First ascent: M. von Kuffner with A. Burgener and
J.P. Ruppen, 15 July, 1890, coming from the Zwischbergenpass and glacier to join the ridge at pt. 3331m. First ascent
of complete ridge as described below: M. Maglin and G. de
Santis, 19 August, 1913. The ridge was reached at the intermediate pt. 3255m. from the Andolla side by R. Gerla with
G.B. Aymonod and L. Marani, 23 July, 1890.

36. From the Andolla hut a small track (not shown on map)
leads to pt. 2466m. marking the foot of the large SE spur of
pt. 3255m. Follow this track in grass and scree until the large
cwm between the latter spur and the spur coming down from
pt. 2861m. opens above. Leave the track and climb into this
cwm, keeping R, and aim for the col, pt. 2803m. in the top
R-hand corner. Reach the col over broken rocks and snow,
where the ascent of the main E ridge starts (2 h.). The ridge
is soon blocked by a steep rock wall; climb this direct (20m.,
III), and continue on the crest with interesting scrambling to
pt. 3178m. Cross this and descend R to the snowfields of the
Zwischbergen glacier. Make a fairly long curving traverse,
down at first then up, round a rock projection from pt. 3255m.
on the ridge above, then round another projection before crossing a bergschrund and climbing snow slopes to rejoin the
ridge on the broad snow dome, pt. 3331m. Follow this, narrowing, to the foot of the final rock ridge (2 h.). Climb the
stepped ridge without incident to a small shoulder nearly half-
way up. (Escape to L possible, up to S ridge). Continue up a
narrow ridge to a large pointed gendarme, turn it on the L
(III) and finish on steep rock directly at the summit (2 h., 6 h.
from Andolla hut).

<u>South-East Face</u>. A classic route though having a smaller
following than the SE spur. An original route on the face,

fairly exposed to stonefall, took a direct line up the shallow central couloir to the summit. III+. G. D. Ferrari and G. Corradi, 18 September, 1896. The more recent Bonacossa route is on sound rock and though hardly less direct is a much better climb. Recommended. 650m. III with short pitches of III+/IV. First ascent: A. Bonacossa and G. Vitale, 6 August, 1947.

37. From the Andolla hut a small track (not shown on map) leads to pt. 2466m. marking the foot of the large SE spur of pt. 3255m. From this pt. continue rising across the opening to a cwm above, on scree and snow, and reach a large flattish moraine hump at the foot of the next spur, which encloses the N branch of the Andolla glacier. From here climb rubble then snow or ice towards the head of the glacier, to below the SE face at c. 3000m. This small glacier can be icy and crevassed in late season (3 h.).

The face below the summit is split by three couloirs, none large but quite distinct. Cross a bergschrund (sometimes awkward) between the first couloir on the L and the second and climb the L side of the rock rib between the two for about 150m. Continue up a short overhanging wall then a dièdre to reach a zone of steep grey slabs. Climb the slabs for 80m. and finish direct a few m. L of the summit (5-6 h., 8-9 h. from Andolla hut).

<u>South-East Spur and South Ridge</u>. The conspicuous buttress descending from pt. 3492m. on the S ridge. By this route the most entertaining part of the main traverse ridge can be done as a finale to a fine scramble up the most popular route on the Italian side of the mtn. Pegs in place for abseiling down the spur. Mainly excellent rock. III+. Recommended. First ascent: A. Bonacossa and A. Malinverno, 24 July, 1941.

38. From the Andolla hut a small track traverses SW along the grassy slopes of the valley to the huts of Alpe Corone (2324m)., but this is difficult to follow in the dark and is not marked on map after crossing the ravine at pt. 2158m. The best plan is to use the higher track from the hut to pt. 2466m., as described in Route 37. From here traverse scree and snow slopes rising only a little, keeping well below the N branch of the Andolla glacier, and work towards the foot of the SE spur. Pass round the foot of the spur to the L (S) side and ascend scree and snow (S branch of Andolla glacier) to the foot of the S subsidiary rib of the spur (c. 2800m., $2\frac{1}{2}$ h.). Climb this prominent rib on pleasant rocks to a step, turn this on the L and return to the crest up a ledge line. Continue on or near the crest with steeper pitches of II and III and a wall of 7m. (III+). The upper part of the ridge is more broken but still steep, up to pt. 3492m. (3 h.). Now follow the S ridge as for Route 35 to the summit ($1\frac{3}{4}$ h., and about $7\frac{1}{2}$ h. from Andolla hut).

PORTJE (PORT) 3295m.

The gap at the foot of the S ridge of the Portjengrat. See Route 35. The Italian side is a steep couloir-chimney, rarely climbed (PD+). The gap is not the lowest point in the main ridge between the Portjengrat and Mittelrück. Closer to the latter is the depression measured as pt. 3228m., at the foot of the N ridge of the Mittelrück.

MITTELRÜCK 3363.1m.

Ital: Pizzo di Loranco. A secondary summit having one of the finest rock climbs in the area on its E spur. Infrequently climbed for itself and always a better mountaineering proposition from the Andolla side. On the Swiss side the summit is easily reached from points on the Rotblatt glacier by the N or S ridges, or by the S flank of the WNW ridge, in about 4 h. from the Almagelleralp inn. First recorded tourist ascent: W. M. Conway, G. Broke and G. H. Rendall with X. Andenmatten, 25 July, 1887.

East Spur (Lago Maggiore-Grat). So called because of the fine view of that distant lake obtained when ascending the ridge. This spur forms a well defined ridge coming down at c. 3300m. from the S ridge of the mtn. some distance from the summit. Its base is marked pt. 2522m., but for some 150m. above this pt. the ridge is without much interest. It is usual to reach the crest from the L(S) side at c. 2700m. The rock is excellent throughout. Probably the finest rock climb in the region. Illogically is it more frequented from the Swiss side because the potential number of expeditions from the Saas valley is much greater; access is fairly easy across the Sonnigpass. IV, 600m. Pegs not necessary. Direct finish, V. Climbed frequently since 1950. Recommended. First ascent: A. Bonacossa with A. Revel, 15 July, 1918. Direct: the guides R. O. and Q. Zurbriggen, 22 September, 1947.

39. From the Andolla hut follow the track to the Alpe Corone huts (2324m.) ($1\frac{1}{2}$ h.). See note in Route 38. From the huts the poor track continues SW and eventually fades in scree (approach to this side of the Sonnigpass). Bear R up to and past the end of the SE spur and reach its crest on your R at c. 2700m. No difficulty (1 h.). Climb the steep narrow ridge ahead, preferably taking pitches direct, which are finer and on better rock than turning them on one side or the other. Numerous short pitches of III and IV, slabs, cracks, chimneys and walls. Continue to a steep headwall; by moving L a line of slanting gangways lead in a steep rising traverse to the S ridge midway between the Sonnigpass and the summit ($3\frac{1}{2}$ h. from start of serious climbing, $4\frac{1}{2}$ h. from Alpe Corone). Finish up the fairly easy ridge, always keeping L to avoid awkward bits on the crest and with some interest on the crest in the last 100m. (30 min., $6\frac{1}{2}$ h. from Andolla hut).

Direct finish: First climb a steep wall trending R on small holds and reach a chimney. Take this on good holds with two awkward overhangs, 32m., cairn. Continue direct on easier rock to the S ridge and follow this in 20 min. to the summit.

Coming from the Almagelleralp inn, the Sonnigpass (q. v.) is traversed to the Italian side, where snow and debris are traversed until the ridge crest can be gained at c. 2700m. as in the approach from the Andolla hut (4-4½ h. from inn to start of serious climbing on ridge; about 8½ h. from inn to summit).

SONNIGPASS 3147m.

Ital: Bocchetta del Bottarello.   Between the Mittelrück and Sonnighorn. Though fairly easy and with some following in the past, this pass is seldom used today except by climbing parties crossing the Portjengrat chain. It is quite fine and interesting for itself, and practical for experienced mtn. walkers. The col is not normally crossed at its lowest pt. but at a place a short distance up the NE ridge of the Sonnighorn. Both sides, F+.

40. Swiss side: From the Almagelleralp inn follow the main track in the valley bed to the third bend at c. 2480m. From here a smaller track continues SE over grassy slopes and rises to the crest of the lateral moraine, on your R, of the Rotblatt glacier. Follow the track on this moraine to near pt. 2798m., then slant R over stones and blocks to reach the glacier at c. 2800m. Ascend the L side of the glacier (open crevasses in late season) and, bearing L, reach its upper snowfield which is crossed SE to the broad snow saddle of the col (3 h.).

41. Italian side, in descent: From the saddle go up towards the Sonnighorn, keeping well L along the rocky rim at the top of cliffs on the Italian side. Down to the L(S) a large ledge line is seen crossing the face below the ridge at c. 3220m. Follow this more or less upwards to a point about 50m. below pt. 3332m. on the ridge above. Now descend the large buttress directly below in zigzags by easy rocks and grassy terraces to the foot, and continue L (NE) under pt. 2761m. to-

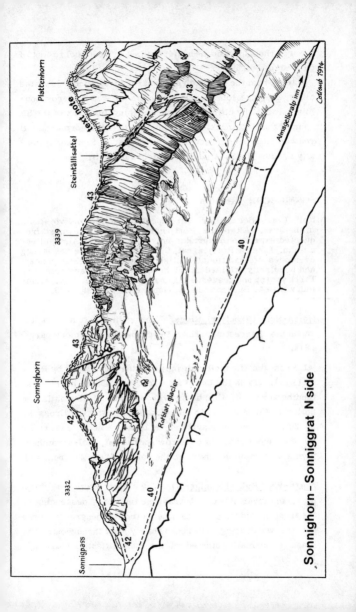

Sonnighorn – Sonniggrat N side

towards the Alpe Corone hut (45 min. -1 h. from col to foot of buttress).

Note: From the col a direct route can be made down the cliffs, keeping L looking out, which emerges in a narrow couloir between the cliffs and rocks forming the flank of the SE spur of the Mittelrück. This is quicker than the normal way if you can find the correct line, discovered in 1950 and generally used by the Saas guides. Pitches of II/III.

SONNIGHORN 3487.2m.

Ital: Pizzo Bottarello. An important summit and viewpoint in the area. After the Portjengrat probably the most frequented expedition undertaken normally from the Almageller-alp inn. Like the Portjengrat, the classic traverse has strong overtones of traditional British mountaineering, in concept and popularity. Mixed climbing of above-average interest. First ascent and traverse generally credited to: A. F. Mummery with A. Burgener and A. Gentinetta, August, 1879.

<u>North-East (Frontier) Ridge</u>. The ordinary route. A fine scramble, interesting. PD+. Descended by Mummery party, 1879.

42. From the Almagelleralp inn reach the Sonnigpass by Route 40 (3 h.). Go up the broad snow ridge to a rock barrier extending across it. Climb a snow groove in this to a small snow hollow and continue up to the rock crest on the L. Cross pt. 3332m. and turn a gendarme ahead by a fine snow crest on its R. The upper ridge is a narrow rock crest, nail-scratched, giving a splendid scramble to the summit (1 h. , 4 h. from inn).

<u>North-West Ridge (Sonniggrat)</u>. The classic route, very popular, and invariably used to traverse the mtn. , descending by the frontier ridge. Not as fine as the Portjengrat traverse but well worth doing. The rock is fairly good throughout. The ridge is normally started at the Steintällisattel (3226m.).

PD+ with short pitches of III, also one section of IV, avoidable. Recommended. First ascent: J. D. James with A. Supersaxo and E. Imseng, 26 July, 1889. Mummery's ascent was by the rather dull SW flank of the mtn.

43. From the Almagelleralp inn follow Route 40 to the Rotblatt glacier, and cross this immediately at c. 2760m. to the opposite (W) side. Then cross a small lateral moraine and go up a steep scree shoot between the end of a rock barrier and the foot of a large rib further L, coming down from a point just L of the Steintällisattel. Climb into the bed of a narrow shelf-like cwm between this rib and the N ridge of the Plattenhorn on your R, over rough ground. Soon slant L on to the broad back of the rib. Follow it usually with some snow to the steeper head slope of the cwm. Slant R away from the rib and climb the head slope direct to the Steintällisattel; route partly cairned (3¼ h.).

From the saddle follow the ridge, soon narrowing in a fine position, to the top of a step. Abseil 12m. to continue the ridge with short pitches of II over pt. 3339m. and some slightly harder in descent over and round small teeth, leading to the snow gap at the foot of the final ridge (1½ h.). It starts with a big step in three tiers; slabs, walls and an exit dièdre, pitches of IV. It is normally avoided by steep rock steps and rising terraces on the R side, rejoining the crest just behind the top of the step. Continue up the sharp crest, cut by many small teeth and gaps which are more or less taken direct to the summit (III). This part of the ridge can also be avoided by making a series of much less sporting traverses down on the R (S) side of the ridge (1¼ h., about 6 h. from inn).

PLATTENHORN 3324m.

The first summit proper of the Sonniggrat. The original traverse of this ridge to the Sonnighorn (Route 43) included the

traverse of this summit, from the Kanziljoch (3189m.), over
the intermediate shoulder of Kanzilti (3308m.) then the Plattenhorn, and so to the Steintällisattel. Enthusiasts might consider this addition to the Sonniggrat-Sonnighorn traverse
worthwhile; some sections of the ridge include pitches of II/
II+ on good rock. Allow an additional 2 h. over the normal
6 h. to reach the Sonnighorn. The rocks at the top of the Wysstal glacier used to reach the Kanziljoch are steeper (II+) than
the head slope of the Steintällisattel. Another alternative is
to climb the N ridge of the Plattenhorn which gives nice slab
pitches of III; some of them can be avoided on the R.

ALMAGELLHORN 3327.2m.

A fine viewpoint, rarely climbed. The only convenient route
from the Almagelleralp inn is the SE ridge from the Kanziljoch (see Plattenhorn above). This is scrambling on good rock
(1 h. from col, 4 h. from inn). The summit can be reached as
a training walk from Saas Almagell village in the main valley,
starting with the Furggstalden chairlift to 1900m. From here
by path to the Chapf chalet (1985m.), then by a track in the
forest to reach the W slopes of the mtn., which are ascended
for some distance before moving R onto the SW ridge which
leads to the top. About $3\frac{1}{2}$ h. from chairlift.

CRESTA DI SAAS

The collective name for the next section of the main frontier
ridge running S from the Sonnighorn to the Latelhorn (Punta
di Saas) (3204m.). It includes several minor peaks and cols.
The Swiss (W) side consists of monotonous slopes of grass,
scree and rock barriers. The Italian (E) side has several fine
cliffs on which fairly recent rock climbs have been made.
Remote access from the hydro-electric lakes high above Ant-
tronapiana.

ANTRONAPASS (PASSO DI SAAS) 2838m.

A major pass across the frontier ridge immediately after the
Latelhorn (Cresta di Saas), from Almagell to Antronapiana.
Though known and used since the Middle Ages, hardly ever
crossed today with the result that the fine path is overgrown
and partly lost. About 4 h. from Almagell, up the Furggtälli
valley, to the pass.

JAZZIHORN (PIZZO CINGINA NORD) 3227m.

An important junction of ridges where the frontier changes course and where the Stelli branch ridge runs N to enclose the Mattmark section of the upper Saas valley on its E side. Short scrambles and climbs on good rock. Access remote.

STELLIHORN 3436m.

The highest summit on the large spur detached from the frontier ridge at the Jazzihorn. Its W and SW slopes dominate the Mattmark barrage. The mtn. is rarely climbed, superb regional view. The best walking route from the barrage is up the Wysstal (poor track) to the Stellipass (3038m.) (3 h.), then by the snowfield of the Nollen glacier, under the NW ridge of the mtn., to the top (another hour).

OFENTALPASS (PASSO DI ANTIGINE) 2835m.

An easy frontier ridge crossing from near the S end of the Mattmark barrage, up the Ofental and down the Antrona valley to Antronapiana.

SPECHHORN (PIZZO DI ANTIGINE) 3189m.

A fine viewpoint lying SE of the Mattmark barrage. From the chalet inn at the S end of the barrage, by the NW ridge, in $3\frac{1}{2}$ h. F/PD.

JODERHORN 3035.7m.

A fairly frequented summit, noted for its view of the E face of Monte Rosa. Reached in 30 min. from the Monte Moropass over large blocks and rough slopes, easier by keeping L on the Swiss side.

MONTE MOROPASS 2868m.

From the Saas valley (Mattmark) to Macugnaga. The lowest point of the ridge is 2846m., situated about 400m. NW of the correct crossing point at 2868m. The former lies directly above the cableway station on the Italian side, and above a small lake.

One of the great pedestrian crossings of the Pennine Alps, known since the Middle Ages, used frequently in more recent times, but with a falling off of interest between 1930 and 1960. The construction of the Mattmark barrage road, the opening of an inn at the S end of the lake on the Swiss side and the public service cableway from Macugnaga to a point only 30 min. from the summit of the pass have revived interest tremendously. When the author's party crossed the pass in 1971 between 9 and 11 am at least 150 people were moving up and down the path in this short time. Notwithstanding the fact that this crossing is one of the most rocky and roughest walking routes in the Pennines, and in poor visability it is quite difficult to follow the correct path. In the upper section there are many false trails and variations, with a profusion of cairns and paint waymarks. Above the cableway on the Italian side are several small narrow cwms filled with huge stones and boulders. Frozen snow patches are frequent and an ice axe is useful. F, both sides.

44. Swiss side: From the Mattmark barrage post bus terminus (restaurant), c. 2180m., follow the lorry road along the W shore of the lake to the S end. Slip road on R to inn (2238m.). Keep L and cross the main stream coming down the Tälli cwm. Follow the good path up the L side of this without possible error, crossing the stream again and rising gradually to a conspicuous zone of slanting rock terraces. The path (and false trails) goes up these fairly directly, cairns and paint flashes, to a scree plain (snowfield), before rising again in a large groove (snow) between slabby ribs to the broad flat opening of the pass (about $2\frac{1}{2}$ h., $1\frac{3}{4}$ h. in descent).

45. Italian side, from cableway station (2810m.), signposts and paint flashes mark the way in a narrow rock strewn valley, first N then E to a contractors building shown on LK25 at the last bend R (E) in the original path from Macugnaga.

Confusing terrain. From the bend continue E up a short narrow valley (snow), then the path bends L(N) and a scramble over rocks or up a snow slope to its L leads to the summit plateau (30 min. from cableway).

From Macugnaga on foot. Start from the Monte Rosa hotel on the L side of the main road going out of the village. The track is well shown on map. Climb in the forest to a junction for the Meccia chalets on the R. Keep L and continue to a junction on the R for the Sonobierg chalets. Keep L again and climb the winding path to the stony valley leading to the pass. Follow this (wearisome) to parallel rock ribs through which the path passes (snow) and enters the desolate upper valley. Near the top the Malnate hut can be seen a short distance to the L (W). Turn R at a sharp bend beside a contractors building and join the approach from the cableway, as above (about 5 h. from Macugnaga, $2\frac{1}{2}$ h. in descent).

Section Two

NEUES WEISSTOR - MISCHABEL

Huts and other mountain bases

Eugenio Sella Hut 3029m.

Rifugio Eugenio Sella. Situated on the Italian approach to the Neues Weisstor pass, on a platform at the top of a promontory dividing the Jazzi and Roffel glaciers. The hut has been prone to damage by avalanches in the past. For this volume of the guide it provides the normal starting point from Italy for climbing the Strahlhorn. Warden, simple restaurant service, places for 50.

46. From the square in Macugnaga (Staffa) go down the main road (bus) to Pecetto di Sopra (1362m.). Keep R and follow a lane through the last houses to a fork (1378m.). Keep R again (L for the Belvedere), cross some pastures and climb a moraine cwm between the stream and the mountainside. When the path leaves the stream, climb a rock spur (cut steps) and descend a little to reach the foot of a grassy gorge with a waterfall on the R (1 h.). Climb zigzags in the gorge (cut steps); in the upper part cross the gorge to a grassy knoll where the path forks. Take the L branch and ascend another grassy gorge (waterfall) to reach the Roffelstafel huts (1905m.) (45 min.). It is not necessary to pass the huts which stand 100m. to the L, below a rocky bank.

Now the path climbs grassy slopes in zigzags, passing to the L of two waterfalls and going up some rocks. More grass then stony slopes and scree lead to snow under the promontory on which the hut stands. Work up to the lower L (W) side of the promontory and ascend under the rocks to the foot of a buttress forming a corner. Slant R (N) round this and climb snow and scree to the hut ($2\frac{1}{2}$ h., $4\frac{1}{2}$ h. from Macugnaga. In descent, 2 h.).

Starting from the Belvedere, at the top of the chairlift, the glacier can be crossed to Alpe Fillar, and a path followed down to a junction with the Macugnaga path at a point slightly above Roffelstafel ($3\frac{1}{2}$ h. from Belvedere to hut).

Mattmark Inn   2238m.

Situated just beyond the S end of the Mattmark barrage, and at the end of the lorry road along the W side of the barrage. About 40 min. walking from the bus terminus below the Mattmark barrage. Restaurant and inn accommodation.

Fluhalp Hotel   2618m.

Hôtel Fluh. A large building situated in a conspicuous position behind the R bank moraine of the Findelen glacier on the normal Zermatt approach to the Rimpfischhorn. Bedrooms and dormitory accommodation, good restaurant service.

47. From Zermatt most parties use the chairlift to Sunnegga, which is 15 min. walk from centre of the resort, and at Sunnegga the lazy can transfer to the first stage of Unterrothorn cableway system and get off at Blauherd. From here the hotel is reached (first by a short descent) in 45 min.

From Sunnegga however, a path (signpost) climbs fairly steeply into a little grass and rock cwm to the E. After exiting to the R it works horizontally across pleasant mountainside, passing below the Blauherd station, then along the S shore of Stellisee before reaching the hotel ($1\frac{3}{4}$ h. from Sunnegga).

The original mule path from Zermatt via Winkelmatten and the Findeln hamlet (up to where it is now a jeep road) takes 3 h. on foot.

Findeln (Findelen) is spelt both ways on the new LK25 map.

<u>Britannia Hut</u> 3030m.

Britanniahütte. The original and now much improved hut built
by subscription among the Association of British Members of
the SAC. Now also the largest club hut in the Mischabel chain
and the most overrun. It has come in for a lot of attention
from summer skiers who are facilitated by the new cableway
systems out of Saas Fee. Situated on the col at the E end of
the Hinter Allalin ridge. Places for 115, warden, restaurant
and waitress service.

48. Direct cableway approach from Saas Fee. To terminus of
the Felskinn cableway, 2991m. From here a large piste in
the snow (almost horizontal) is followed SE across the Chessjen
(Kessjen) glacier, passing just above the Egginerjoch
(2989m.), to the hut in 45 min.

   The traditional afternoon walking route from Saas Fee passes
round the E side of the Mittaghorn-Egginer rock ridge. The
first part of this approach is now facilitated by the Plattjen
cableway, to the hotel of the same name at 2570m. From here
on foot: a good path crosses a shoulder (large cairn) and contours below the Mittaghorn to the S and SW, under its steep
rocks (cut steps, rails). After crossing the Meiggertal and
passing a hut, Heidefridhof (2764m.) the path drops a little to
the moraine and snow of the Chessjen glacier. Climb up this
directly to the S and reach the hut on the skyline ($2\frac{1}{2}$ h. from
cableway).

<u>Täschalp Inn</u> 2170m.

This small inn is noted for its hospitality. Restaurant and
simple hotel service. Useful for climbing the Leiterspitzen.
A road reaches the inn from Täsch (taxi service, if required).
On foot, see below.

Täsch Hut 2701m.

Täschhütte. Situated on a grassy shelf at the S foot of the Rot-grat of the Alphubel. Places for 40, resident warden, simple restaurant service. There is a road to Täschalp and a rough jeep road to not far below the hut.

49. From the Täsch village it is now quicker to walk up the road to the upper valley, where the Täschalp inn is reached in $1\frac{3}{4}$ h. Taxis can be hired at the railway station.

From Zermatt (apart from taking a train down to Täsch, then a taxi to the inn) walk down the main road towards Täsch to a large signpost on the R, pointing the way to the traverse path which goes through the woods above the main valley (30 min.). Follow this small path, fairly steeply at first, then in long and almost level sections to a final junction with the old and large mule path coming up from Täsch. Five-bar gate. Follow this to a junction with the new road, just below where it levels out near the bed of the valley. Continue along the road to Täschalp ($2\frac{1}{4}$ h., $2\frac{3}{4}$ h. from Zermatt).

From the Täschalp inn the old footpath has been erased by debris in making the new jeep road. Follow the latter which is quite steep, and at a prominent junction in the lower section go R. Near the end of the long traverse section high above the valley floor, and soon after passing a block of chalets built on a split level below the road (shown on map), find a small track which forks L (turning circle for jeeps) (1 h.). Follow the track in wide zigzags to the hut, which is reached from the R (30 min., $1\frac{1}{2}$ h. from Täschalp, $3\frac{1}{4}$ h. from Täsch on foot, $4\frac{1}{4}$ h. from Zermatt on foot).

Note: hut enlarged to nearly twice former size in June 1974.

Längfluh Hotel 2870m.

Hôtel Längflue. The much visited rock island jutting into the Fee glacier which is reached by cableway directly from Saas Fee (two stages). The hotel has dormitories for 80, rest-

aurant and snack bar. Those who prefer to walk from Saas
Fee have an excellent mule path which is easily followed from
the map. Midway restaurant at Spielboden. 3 h. on foot from
Saas to hotel.

Mischabeljoch Bivouac 3860m.

Really a small hut, situated just above the Mischabeljoch
(3851m.), on the rocks of the Täschhorn. Fully equipped,
10 places maximum, no warden, no cooking stove (take your
own). Melt snow for water.
  The Mischabeljoch is the most serious of the practical glacier
passes across the Mischabel chain; access to the hut is therefore not easy. It is difficult to grade the approaches because
the main problem is the variable state of the glaciers, which
are generally bad on both sides of the pass; they can be dangerous in the late afternoon or after fresh snowfall. Both sides
at least PD, normally PD+ on Saas side. Parties sometimes
choose to traverse the Alphubel to reach the pass and hut;
this procedure avoids all complications with crevasses. More
details about the pass itself appear under its own heading.

50. Zermatt side. From the rear of the Täsch hut follow the
obvious traverse path to the NW. This excellent path goes up
into the Tälli cwm, between the two branches of the lower Rotgrat. Reach a stone circle construction of large spikes and
cairns on the N ridge branch (Wissgrat), c. 3140m. (1¼ h.).
Leave the continuation track and in a few paces to the N(L) find
a stone staircase in large blocks leading down to the S branch
of the Weingarten glacier, which is covered with moraine.
Make a descending traverse NE and cross it (no path, a few
cairns, loose), rising slightly in the same direction, and finally
cross a short steep moraine to the narrow branch between the
W ridge of the N summit of the Alphubel (base pt. 3242m.)
and a rock wall supporting the main branch of the Weingarten
glacier, at a higher level above. This wall has a nick in its
crest at the R-hand (upper) end, pt. 3481m. Climb over moraine to the centre foot of the wall (45 min.).
  Either: climb fairly sound red rocks, starting somewhat L

94

of the centre, by a rising movement L, then R and straight up, and finally R, finishing on a low rock crest beside the glacier (moves of II/II+, many variations possible, 15 min.). Then go along the rock crest and in the icy gutter between it and the icefall to your L, up to where the rocks rise steeply in a slabby ridge. Pt. 3481m., 15 min.

Or: Climb under the rock wall to the R(E) and go up a snow slope into a loose, narrow couloir (round a corner) which rises to the nick of pt. 3481m. During the early hours of morning this couloir is probably the best way; the last 10m. are nearly vertical (abseil in descent) (30 min.).

Now above the worst part of the icefall, traverse on to the glacier, rising slightly to reach its centre. In practice it is generally best to work up the centre at first, before moving across to the far L side. Several huge crevasses split the glacier from side to side and the problem is finding safe bridges; the crevasses usually involve long detours to the L or R. Finally climb near the L side of the glacier over easy snow slopes to a small bergschrund under the col; turn this on the L and reach the small snow saddle. The hut is up on rocks to the L (NW) ($1\frac{1}{2}$-$2\frac{1}{4}$ h., 4-$4\frac{3}{4}$ h. from Täsch hut. In descent, $2\frac{1}{4}$-3 h.).

51. Saas side. From the Längfluh hotel a track leads in a few min. to the glacier. At first work to the R (SW) and climb in the wide glacier cwm which lies below the long rock barrier coming down from the Alphubel; skitow and skiing markers. The foot of this barrier is pt. 2989m. Immediately to the L(S) of this pt. there is a long couloir, part snow, part rock, slanting SW up to the glacier terrace above the barrier. Climb the couloir as directly as possible to pt. 3358.9m. at its head (1 h.). When there is a lot of snow in the couloir, climb its bed for some 15m. only, then go along a vague horizontal ledge line to the R and climb the parallel rock rib. Soon move further R into the gutter between the rocks and the glacier on the R; then at 3200m. climb the glacier itself.

Above the couloir climb steep snow to the SW and reach the glacier terrace at c. 3550m. Now cross to the W and reach the foot of the big slope below the Mischabeljoch ($1\frac{1}{2}$ h.). Cross the bergschrund, sometimes large, and climb the steep snow/ice slope on a diagonal line to the R. The lowest point of the col is to the R, under the rocks of the Täschhorn, where the hut is situated (1 h., $3\frac{3}{4}$ h., but allow up to $4\frac{1}{2}$ h. In descent, 2-3 h.).

Dom Hut 2940m.

Domhütte. A fairly new hut, situated on the lower moraines of the Festi glacier, and above a large rock wall overlooking Randa. The approach is a noted "slog"; in fact the path is excellent but rather steep and rocky. Resident warden, places for 40, simple restaurant service.

52. From Randa station go along the road to Zermatt to a fork leading back through the village, to the NW. Follow the lane (signposts) then a path across meadows and cross the Dorf stream. Now climb many steep zigzags in the Larchberg forest to open pastures where the path eases a little. By more zigzags work L then R to the first rock section up a grassy buttress; cut steps with a few rails and old pegs up to pt. 2503m. Reach a section which goes L to another large rock step. The path climbs this with interest to blocks and scree on the L side of the rock face, near its top. Continue up the path, past the old hut to the new, which is not visible till the last moment ($4\frac{1}{2}$-5 h. from Randa).

Mischabel Hut 3329m.

Mischabelhütte. An old hut, situated on the rocks dividing the Hohbalm and Fall glaciers, directly above and to the W of Saas

Fee. The hut belongs to the AACZ, so there are reduced rates for SAC members, but not others. The walk up is a noted "effort". Warden, places for 60, simple restaurant service.

53. From the church in Saas Fee follow the well marked footpath to the W, cross the Torren stream then go up the first series of endless zigzags to where the angle eases temporarily on the Schönegge shoulder (2448.6m.). Continue in the same direction up more zigzags, climbing below the Distelhorn then up scree and rocky ground on the R side of the Fall glacier. The path steepens and reaches the short rock ridge leading to the hut (4 h. from Saas Fee, $1\frac{3}{4}$ h. in descent).

Route by using Hannigalp-Mällig cableway. From Saas Fee take this one stage lift to its terminus at c. 2400m. From here an improved and in parts newly engineered path makes a descending traverse SW then NW round a rocky shoulder of the Mällig mountain, then the Torren stream is crossed at c. 2275m. The path now contours S, rising a little all the way to a series of zigzags under the Distelhorn, to join the direct walking route from Saas Fee just below the top of the Schönegge shoulder (2448.6m.) (1 h. from cableway terminus). Continue to the hut, as above (2 h., 3 h. in all from cableway).

Bordier Hut   2886m.

Bordierhütte. Situated on a moraine terrace above the R bank of the Ried glacier and at the W foot of the Kl. Bigerhorn. Warden, places for 52, restaurant service.

54. The hut is reached from St. Niklaus (railway), from where a fairly frequent bus service goes to Grächen (1619m.) and Ried (1659m.). From Ried follow the signposted footpath beside the water supply channel, then cross the Ried stream in a ravine and rise to the junction with the direct path coming from St. Niklaus (1739m.). After a section in the forest the path reaches the Alpja chalets (2099m.) in a moraine valley. Further up, the path goes along the moraine crest to some zigzags, before reaching the true L bank of the glacier at c. 2770m. Cross the glacier (30 min.) to the other (E) side, large cairn, with the hut standing above it. The crevasses can be troublesome (rope advisable). Continue up the path in moraine and rocks to the hut ($3\frac{1}{2}$-4 h. from Ried).

PART III

Rimpfischhorn group

Neues Weisstor to Alphubeljoch

NEUES WEISSTOR (PASS) 3499m.

In the Weissgrat, between the Neue Weisstorspitze (Punte del Neues Weisstor) and the Cima di Jazzi. The most direct and easiest pass between Zermatt and Macugnaga, at the lowest point in this section of the frontier ridge. The Zermatt side consists of huge uneven glacier slopes with several but not serious crevasse zones, F+. The Italian side is blocked by a large cornice, below which is a somewhat dangerous couloir. This "direct" route is not used today, for which there is a convenient variant (Passage Jacchini), PD-.
    First tourist traverse: Walters and Blomfield with J. and S. Zumtaugwald, 29 August, 1856.

55. Zermatt side. Start either from the Fluhalp hotel or from the top of the Stockhorn cableway. The former is longer and bedevilled by masked crevasses between 3000-3200m. Otherwise it is straightforward and with intelligent use of the map requires no special directions. In good snow conditions one of the finest glacier tours in the Alps, recommended. Reach the frontier somewhat L(N) of the lowest point of the pass, at the top of the first low shoulder on the ridge rising to the Neue Weisstorspitze (about 4 h. from Fluhalp, $2\frac{1}{4}$ h. in descent).

From the Stockhorn terminus follow the easy ridge to the Stockhorn and continue down to the Stockhornpass (3394m.) (1 h.). Continue up the broad glacier spur to the SE, and only at c. 3500m. leave it and contour slopes to the E and N in order to round the NW glacier shoulder of the Cima di Jazzi at c. 3600m. This high contouring movement avoids large crevasses lower down. On the N side snow slope of this mountain, drop down before turning E(R) to reach the pass ($1\frac{1}{2}$ h., $2\frac{1}{2}$ h. from Stockhorn terminus, about same time in reverse direction).

56. Italian side. Passage Jacchini. From the Eugenio Sella hut return along the hut approach for c. 50m. to a track forking R and leading on to a buttress overlooking the hut to the WNW. This buttress marks the S edge of the Roffel glacier and the track on it is clearly marked on map. Climb along the shoulder crest of the buttress, beside the glacier, to where the track is lost in rocks and snow. Continue in the same direction, either on the buttress or glacier slopes just to the R. A steeper snow slope leads to a snow shoulder, which is climbed to mid-height. Now slant L in the direction of the pass; cross a natural break in the rocks and using ledges and terraces reach the frontier ridge immediately above and to the R of the lowest point of the pass. From here descend a short snow slope to the pass ($1\frac{1}{2}$ h., 1 h. in descent).

NEUE WEISSTORSPITZE 3639m. 3641m.

Ital: Punte del Neues Weisstor. The higher point on the ridge to the N is relatively insignificant. The lower (main) point dominates the N side of the Neues Weisstor pass (see above). Climbable from the Weissgrat snowfields, or by steep loose rocks directly above the Italian side exit ledges to the pass.

SCHWARZBERGHORN 3609m.

Ital: Corno Nero di Macugnaga. An insignificant summit at an important junction of ridges. The point at which the Mischabel chain commences (strictly speaking the Schwarzberg Weisstor pass which adjoins the summit), leaving the frontier ridge at this point and running N entirely into Switzerland. See next entry.

SCHWARZBERG WEISSTOR (PASS) 3535m.

The lowest point in the almost level ridge between the Schwarz-berghorn and the base of the Strahlhorn. At this point the col is not practicable, having an unpleasant rockface on the E (Saas) side. When this part of the ridge is crossed as a pass parties must go over the Schwarzberghorn (easy). An old crossing, rarely used today. A full description for Spring skiers appears in the "High Level Route" guide by Eric Roberts.

STRAHLHORN 4190.1m.

This is the most southerly of the great summits of the Mischa-bel chain which divides the Zermatt and Saas valleys. The mtn. is climbed quite frequently from Saas, rather less from Zer-matt and Macugnaga. From Zermatt the route over the Adler-horn is popular among British parties. The Italian route is the most interesting, and this can be joined by Zermatt parties without making a big detour. Altogether, climbed less fre-quently than the Rimpfischhorn.
  First ascent: E.J. Grenville and C. Smyth with F.J. And-enmatten and   U. Lauener, 15 August, 1854. First winter and ski ascent: H. Hoek and E. Schottelius with the guides Tännler and Moor, 31 December, 1901.

West-North-West Ridge (Adlerpass).

West-North-West Ridge (Adlerpass). The usual route from Zermatt and Saas. The ridge is a broad snow hump, easy but crevassed. The Saas approach is F, the Zermatt is PD-. First ascensionists.

57. From the Fluhalp hotel take a good path across rocks then a level plain to a small lake; fork (15 min.). Take the R branch up on to the crest of the lateral moraine; follow this for 30 min., then descend to the ice of the Findelen glacier, which leads to where the Adler glacier joins the main ice stream. (Alternatively, if the crevasses are wide, continue along the moraine and rocks above the side of the glacier, and finally use a large moraine ledge to reach the glacier at c. 2850m.). At this point the glacier is usually half dry and half snow covered; finding a way through the junction can be problematical. Keep close to the L side, using scree slopes above pt. 3001m. before joining the higher snowfield. Now keep R and reach the foot of the col. The final slope of snow or ice is steep; slant up it from L to R, below a bergschrund and beside the Rimpfischhorn rocks in a sort of gully to reach the Adlerpass (4 h. , $2\frac{3}{4}$ h. in descent). An hour can be lost at the junction when the crevasses are bad.

58. From the Britannia hut you can see all the route to the Adlerpass and the summit. A small track drops obliquely SW over scree to the Hohlaub glacier. Cross this in a big curve from W to S and reach at the same level a snowy saddle (3105m.) on the R of rock islet pt. 3148m. A slight descent on the other side leads to the Allalin glacier. Climb its R(N) side, along the foot of the rockface of the Allalinhorn, to reach the upper glacier plateau. Cross this SSW, later bearing SW towards the Rimpfischhorn wall, then up the glacier cwm to the Adlerpass (3 h. , $1\frac{3}{4}$ h. in descent).

59. From the Adlerpass (3789m.) climb somewhat L up the large rounded snow spur of the mtn., to a small shoulder (3954m.). Above this some large crevasses cut the slope which is otherwise easy. Continue straight up to a few rocks at the summit. This section is bad for route finding in poor visibility (1 h. , 5 h. from Fluhalp, 4 h. from Britannia hut).

<u>West-South-West Ridge (over Adlerhorn)</u>. This route has a certain following among British climbers and can be recommended. The glacier at the foot of the ridge can be troublesome, and the way up to the crest of the ridge is variable. PD. First ascent not traced.

60. From Fluhalp hotel start as for Route 57. Either ascend the Adler glacier to above its complicated junction, then cross

102

the glacier SE, above the Strahlchubel rognon (3222m.), to reach the WSW ridge above its foot; or pass below the rognon and reach the foot of the ridge proper. Either way is confused by open and partly concealed crevasses. On the latter approach you must go up a loose rock slope between the foot of the ridge and a sérac step further L to reach the easy slopes crossed by the former approach. From the snow climb up the side of the ridge to its crest behind rock knoll pt. 3421m. Now follow the rock crest, loose but easy to an obvious shoulder. The ridge becomes snowy; trend L then R and finish up a steep snow slope to the summit of the Adlerhorn (3988m.) (4½ h.). From here follow the pleasant snow ridge towards the Strahlhorn, over a saddle (c. 3920m.) and up a continuation ridge, broad at first then narrower at the top, to a forepeak (4128m.). A final snow slope on the R leads to the summit (1¼ h., about 6 h. from Fluhalp).

<u>South-South-East Ridge.</u> Above the Schwarzberg Weisstor pass an escarpment is formed by the E rock wall of the mtn. and its terraced S flank. The resulting edge rises in two steps and provides the most interesting climb on the mtn. It is the normal route from the Eugenio Sella hut; Zermatt based parties can reach it by taking the approach to the Neues Weisstor (Route 55). Recommended, mixed climbing, safe and sure, AD. Comparable in standard, interest and character with the Breithorn Triftjigrat. First known ascent: A. Daglio and A. Sabbadini, 7 September, 1925.

61. From the Eugenio Sella hut follow Route 56 to the Neues Weisstor pass, then contour N below the frontier ridge to the lowest dip in the vicinity of the Schwarzberg Weisstor, at the foot of the ridge (3535m.) (2½ h.). This point is reached from the Fluhalp hotel in 3¾ h. Cross snow to the N, then a bergschrund, and climb a snow funnel at the narrowest point in the rock barrier of the first step. The funnel is followed by a steep snow/ice slope leading to the glacier terrace above. Ascend the terrace in the direction of the summit, then slant R to reach the foot of the second step at pt. 3883m. where it is girdled by a large snow ledge which crosses the entire width of the E face at c. 3900m. Between the glacier terrace and this ledge the rock step forms a prominent angle (ridge); climb its crest on sound rocks with short difficulties and finish on an upper shoulder(4143m.). This section can be quite serious in conditions of fresh snow. Now climb to the W up easy snow slopes to the summit (3 h. from Schwarzberg Weisstor pass, $5\frac{1}{2}$ h. from Eugenio Sella hut, $7\frac{1}{2}$ h. from Fluhalp).

62. Descent. It is quicker and easier to descend by Route 60 to within a short distance of the saddle (c. 3920m.) between the Strahlhorn and Adlerhorn. Leave the ridge at this point, before the saddle, and go down an obvious rock rib slanting L(S) to the glacier terrace; steep slope and bergschrund to finish. Cross the glacier terrace ESE to the top of a rock rib (3807m.) which flanks the true R bank of an ice couloir in the lower step. The head of another rib forming the L bank is also clearly visible, while to the R are séracs. Climb down the R-hand rib to the main glacier below. PD ($1\frac{1}{4}$ h. in descent, 2 h. in ascent). This descent route is about an hour quicker in ascent compared with the proper SSE ridge.

63. <u>East Face</u>. Several routes have been made on this the most remote side of the mtn. The main triangular wall below the forepeak (4143m.) is about 750m. high. It is cut horizontally at c. 3900m. (about 500m. up the face) by a large, steeply sloping horizontal snow terrace. This wall was climbed directly by L. George and V. Russenberger in two separate sessions from a bivouac base at the foot of the wall on 3 and 6 August, 1951. TD, V, upper section III/IV. 10 h. climbing time. Good and bad rock. Probably unrepeated. (Alpinisme, No. 107, 1954).

The approach is from the Mattmark barrage via the Schwarz-bergalp (2372m.), and path to the L bank lateral moraine of the Schwarzberg glacier. The moraine is followed until the N branch of the glacier can be reached on the R, which leads with crevasses to the foot of the face at c. 3400m. (4 h.).

FLUCHTHORN 3790.5m.

A large snow dome on the NE spur of the Strahlhorn. No climbing interest, frequented by Spring skiers.

ADLERPASS 3789m.

A classic glacier pass between the Strahlhorn and Rimpfisch-horn, once the most popular way of going from Saas to Zermatt and vice versa. The troublesome glacier on the Zermatt side has led to other passes being adopted, but both sides are frequented to approach routes up the Strahlhorn. PD-. See Routes 57 and 58. First tourist traverse: M. Ulrich, G. Studer and G. Lauterburg with J. Madutz, F. Andenmatten and F. J. Anthamatten, 9 August, 1849. First traverse on ski: A. von Martin and Dr. Rumpelt with the guides O. Supersaxo and Kronig, 2 April, 1910.

RIMPFISCHHORN 4198.9m.

A very popular mtn., climbed often from Zermatt and Saas. It ranks as an intermediate exercise in preparation for either higher mtns. or harder climbing at a similar altitude. It tends to be used as a training climb, but many people will find the effort too great in this respect. The approaches are fairly long and monotonous. The simple character of this mtn. will be gravely affected if the Feechopf cableway project is realised.
  First ascent: Leslie Stephen and R. Liveing with Melchoir Anderegg and J. Zumtaugwald, 9 September, 1859. First winter ascent: Hermann Woolley with G. and J. Taugwalder, Jnr., 17 January, 1893. First ski ascent: Marcel Kurz and W. Odermatt, 31 March, 1912.

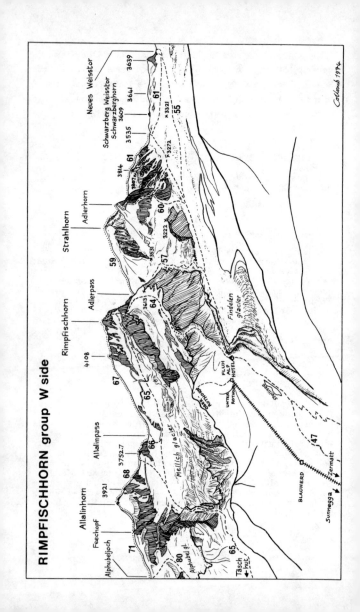

RIMPFISCHHORN group W side

Alphubeljoch Feechopf Allalinhorn Allalinpass Rimpfischhorn Adlerpass Strahlhorn Adlerhorn Schwarzberg Weisstor Neues Weisstor

3921 3752.7 4108 3814 3535 3609 3641 3639

71 68 66 67 65 64 59 57 60 61 55 61

3613 3531 3222 3321 3272

Mellich glacier Alphubel gl. Findelen glacier

UNTERROTHORN FLUH ALP HOTEL STELLISEE

BLAUHERD Sunnegga Zermatt → Täsch → hut.

80 65 47

Collomb 1974

West-South-West Ridge (Rimpfischwänge). The ordinary route from Fluhalp, a long dull approach with more interest at the finish. PD-. First ascensionists.

64. From the Fluhalp hotel take the main footpath E to a tiny lake. The path splits. Follow the L branch along the N side of the lake, then go up a grassy shoulder with rocks (cairns and paint flashes). Reach more level ground which becomes covered with scree and boulders; climb up gradually along the R side of this zone, at the edge of a stony cwm filled with large blocks (Pfulwe). Gradually bear L and go up a shaly slope (snow) to the West Längfluejoch (3155m.) at the ESE foot of the Spitzi Flue (2 h.). Care is need to keep on the small track in this section which is easily lost in the dark.

On the other side of the col make an almost horizontal traverse over scree and snow to the NE, round a corner, then make a rising traverse SSE to arrive at the broad saddle of the East Längfluejoch (3270m.) on the E side of the small summit called Pfulwe (3314m.). Climb the broad ridge ahead over a series of snow/ice and rock humps; one can climb almost anywhere. Finally reach a narrowing where an easy snow ridge rises to a rock band blocking the way. In the line of the ridge climb the rocks by twisting L and R (traces of path) to the snow cap above, where a steep slope leads to the glacier dome (4009m.) (2 h.). Cross this and descend to a broad saddle (Rimpfischsattel) at the foot of a snow slope and the twin rock turrets of the mtn., neither of which is the summit. Climb a triangular snow slope and near the top slant L to reach the rocks of the L-hand spur, about one third of the way up to its summit. A rake slanting from R to L leads to the crest of the spur, then climb its pleasant rocks (bits of II) to the forepeak. Descend into a gap, generally rock and easy but sometimes a narrow corniced snow crest, and scramble to the next top, the true summit (1 h., 5 h. from Fluhalp).

E SIDE

Strahlhorn   Rimpfischhorn   Allalinhorn   Feechopf

71 Alphubeljoch

Feejoch

48

Britannia hut

Allalinpass

3837

70

3140

66   ★3051

67   Allalinpass

4096

58   3620

Adlerpass

59

3954

Fluchhorn

4443   63

61   3906

Schwarzberg Weisstor

3535 ★

3577 ★

3161 ★

65. From the Täsch hut. Follow the traverse path SE to where it joins a lower path climbing E under the rocks of the Vor der Wand. The path is good all the way up to where it brings you to the edge of the Mellich glacier at c. 3300m. Cross this, keeping L to avoid a few crevasses. On nearing the Allalinpass ($2\frac{3}{4}$ h.), curve S and cross a large glacier terrace below the N ridge of the mtn. Rise slightly and cross a narrow snow rib at c. 3640m. Continue at the same height along the terrace and skirt the foot of a rock rib 3662m. The terrace rises to a glacier cwm which is climbed SE then S to the broad saddle (Rimpfischsattel) between the summit rocks and pt. 4009m. ($1\frac{1}{2}$ h.), where the Fluhalp route is joined (1 h., $5\frac{1}{4}$ h. from Täsch hut).

From Britannia hut (Allalinpass). The usual route from the Saas side, which joins the two previous routes at the foot of the summit towers. PD-. First ascent by this approach, before 1915.

66. From the Britannia hut follow Route 58 as for the Adlerpass, as far as the middle plateau of the Allalin glacier at c. 3300m. Now climb a crevassed branch WSW to snowfields forming the broad saddle of the Allalinpass (3564m.) (1 h., $2\frac{1}{2}$ h. from hut). Traverse slightly upwards to the SW and join the Täsch hut route at c. 3640m. on crossing the snow rib ($2\frac{1}{2}$ h., 5 h. from Britannia hut).

North Ridge. The most interesting route on the mtn., usually descended in making a traverse from Fluhalp to Täsch hut; clearly other combinations are possible. The ridge is a regular crest with a number of rounded rock towers, preceded by the pointed Grand Gendarme (4108m.), with a uniform snow/ice slope falling below this to the Allalinpass. PD+. First ascent: G. A. Passingham with F. Imseng and L. Zurbriggen, 1878.

67. Start from the Allalinpass, reached from the Täsch or Britannia huts by Routes 65 or 66 respectively, 3 h. or 2½ h. Climb the wide snow spur to the S, of uniform steepness, to where it narrows to a fine crest and abuts the Grand Gendarme (1½ h.). The gendarme is normally turned on the L, across steep broken rocks, then up a short chimney into a gap on its upper side. It can be traverse on the crest by making two abseils into the gap. (In ascent, i.e. reverse, two pitches of IV and one of III, good rock). The ridge ahead rises progressively in a series of rocky humps and small gendarmes separated by rock or snow saddles. In general the gendarmes can be traversed on the crest, with flanking movements of a few m. and no great difficulty. The linking snow crests are usually sharp and can be corniced; conditions vary. The last tower (summit) is higher than the rest and rises in a series of walls with chimneys and cracks. Climb direct to a final vertical pitch. Move slightly L of the crest and go up a narrow vertical chimney (12m.), which of often verglassed. Arrive directly at the summit (2¼ h. , about 4 h. from Allalinpass, 7 h. from Täsch hut, 6½ h. from Britannia hut).

PFULWE 3314m.
SPITZI FLUE 3317m.
SCHWARZGRAT 3267m.
OBER AND UNTER ROTHORN 3415m. 3103. 4m.

These secondary rock peaks extend from the Längfluejoch reached by Route 64 at the end of the Rimpfischwänge, as a ridge flanking the N side of the Findelen glacier, towards Zermatt. The rock is better than appearances suggest and there are several short, satisfying training climbs on the Spitzi Flue and Schwarzgrat. The other two are easy but tedious slopes of scree and broken rock. The approach to the ridge is combed with paths (many more than those shown on map); because these are short climbers can work out their own routes.

The Unterrothorn is reached by cableway. From its terminus the path to the top of the Oberrothorn (once a classic training walk from Zermatt) has been much improved.

ALLALINPASS 3564m.

Between the Rimpfischhorn and Allalinhorn, the easiest and oldest known glacier pass from Saas to Zermatt. On a time and distance basis the Alphubeljoch is a shorter crossing, because of the Längfluh cableway. Magnificent glacier scenery. Both sides, F. See Routes 65 and 66. First tourist traverse: E. H. Michaelis with guides, 11 September, 1828. First crossed on ski by the guide brothers Supersaxo in March 1911.

ALLALINHORN 4027.4m.

A much trodden mtn. with a reputation for being easier than the Rimpfischhorn and Alphubel; no real comparison can be made because the state of the glaciers varies from year to year. It is abused in some circles and dismissed as a "ski peak", but gives pleasant climbing by any route. The projected cableway to its Feechopf satellite, should it be built, will ruin the mountaineering interest.

First ascent: E. L. Ames with F. J. Andenmatten and a member of the Imseng family, 28 August, 1856. First ski ascent: A. Hurter and M. Stahel with O. and O. Supersaxo, 1 April, 1907.

<u>South-West Ridge</u>. The ordinary route from the Britannia hut, pleasant, interesting and quite feasible in bad conditions. Equally approachable from the Täsch hut. F+. First ascensionists.

68. From the Britannia or Täsch huts reach the Allalinpass by Routes 66 (2½ h.) or 65 (3 h.). From the col you can climb to a gap in the ridge behind a gendarme, then follow the crest, rocks and snow, over pt. 3752.7m. to a small snow saddle (3734m.) beyond. However, it is much quicker to go round the foot of the ridge to the W and climb the W flank up to the snow saddle (30 min.). (Coming from the Täsch hut it is not necessary to start from the col). From the saddle climb the snow ridge to some grey rocks, which are turned on the R, then follow a line of ledges slanting up this E side of the ridge. Regain the crest when it becomes snow again, above the rocks. Climb direct towards a rock shoulder at the top of this section (3921m.), which is conveniently turned on the R by a snow slope. Arrive at the summit snow dome and reach the summit ridge at its R-hand (SE) end. This ridge of snow or ice is narrow and leads to the highest point on rocks in a few min. (1 h., 1½ h. from Allalinpass, 4 h. from Britannia hut, 4½ h. from Täsch hut).

<u>From the North (Feejoch)</u>. This is the Längfluh route and the easiest way to the summit. There are a number of big crevasses below the col. F. First ascent: Leslie Stephen, W. F. Short, F. W. Jacomb and C. Fischer with F. J. Andenmatten, M. Anthamatten, P. Taugwalder and J. Kronig, 1 August, 1860.

69. From the Längfluh hotel go out on to the glacier to the S (L) and enter the broad glacier cwm on this side. Climb due S, keep well clear of séracs around the rognon pt. 3173.7m. and work up the centre of the wide glacier field. At 3200m. the slope steepens a little; bear L then R to avoid crevasses. More large crevasses cut the slope and detours are usually necessary. Continue as directly as possible to the Feejoch (3826m.) (3 h.). From the col climb the broad snow shoulder to the E and reach a snowfield below the summit ridge. Cross below the summit and reach this ridge at the R-hand end; then go along it to the summit (30 min., 3½ h. from Längfluh hotel).

70. <u>East-North-East Ridge (Hohlaubgrat)</u>. This ridge provides the most direct route from the Britannia hut. Not climbed much, recommended, PD. The way is obvious; there is a rock

barrier not far below the summit, which is climbed by a ledge of rotten rocks (3¼ h. to summit). Descended by H. Dübi with A. and P. Supersaxo, 27 July, 1882.

<u>By traverse of Feechopf</u>. A minor classic traverse and popular with British parties. Recommended. See also remarks in preamble to mtn. F+. First ascent and traverse: J. Curtis-Leman with J. Moser and J. M. Kronig, 28 July, 1883.

71. From the Täsch hut or Längfluh hotel reach the Alphubeljoch (3782m.) by Routes 79 (3 h.) or 80 (2½ h.). From the col go up snow to the SE, turning the snow hump pt. 3846m. on the L, and reach the summit of the Feechopf (3888m.). Continue along a sharp rock crest, generally mixed with snow or ice. This can be delicate and exposed and its teeth should be climbed direct (no difficulty); if there is a lot of snow the ridge may be corniced on the R(S). Reach the Feejoch (1 h.) and join Route 69 to the summit (30 min., about 1½ h. from Alphubeljoch, 4½ h. from Täsch hut, 4 h. from Längfluh hotel).

FEEJOCH 3826m.

A minor col between the Allalinhorn and Feechopf, rarely if ever used as a pass between Saas and Zermatt because of a steep rock wall on its S side, loose rocks of grade II. Reached from the N side and its head crossed by trade routes up the Allalinhorn.

FEECHOPF 3888m.

A NW satellite of the Allalinhorn, invariably crossed as a traverse to reach the latter. See Route 71. The summit is threatened with a cableway project which consists of extending the Felskinn line to pt. 3460m. on the Mittel Allalin (NE) ridge of the Allalinhorn, and from there across the glacier to the Feechopf.

EGGINER 3366.6m.

A conspicuous rock mtn. above Saas Fee with some of the most popular practice climbs in the district. It is joined to the Mittaghorn by a fine ridge, and all the main routes are nail scratched. With the advent of the Plattjen and Felskinn cable-ways, treated as a day's outing from Saas Fee. First ascent by chamois hunters.

South-East Side. The ordinary route, a convenient way down for any destination after climbing the mtn. There is a small broken track all the way, not shown on map. PD-.

72. From the Plattjen cableway terminus follow the approach route (48) to the Britannia hut, to Heidefridhof (2764m.). A small track forks R, under the W ridge and takes rough slopes between two rock bands until it meets a subsidiary ridge coming down from the S ridge of the mtn. Go up this ridge, turn a rock wall on the R and reach a large scree or snow band running back across the SE side of the mtn. The vague track goes up this steeply to the upper rock wall, which is taken as directly as possible to the summit ($3\frac{1}{2}$ h. from Plattjen).

From the Britannia hut descend the same hut approach route over the Chessjen glacier; soon slant L and finish off the glacier more to the L. Contour moraine and scree to a terrace slanting R which is followed R to the foot of the subsidiary ridge mentioned above ($2\frac{1}{2}$ h. to summit).

73. East Ridge. Approached as for the previous route. After a scrappy first half, the second gives good climbing on sound rock with two steep sections, III. E.R. Blanchet, 1921.

South-South-West Ridge. This twisting ridge rises above the Egginerjoch (2989m.), first in a big step, in two parts, up to a shoulder (3240m.), then in two smaller steps to the summit. A trade route, worn smooth in places. Good rock, II, with many variations.

74. From the Britannia hut descend the approach route across the Chessjen glacier towards the Felskinn cableway and reach the Egginerjoch below (20 min.). Climb on the crest to the foot of a vertical tower. Traverse R and reach the top of the tower by two nice open pitches. Go along a short ridge to the next riser. Climb this L of the crest, steeply upwards, to a large scree recess. Go into the back of the recess and exit L, so turning overhanging rocks which ring its head. A short scramble leads to the shoulder pt. 3242m. (1 h.). Go along the broad ridge with snow patches to a small tower. Climb this fairly direct, first just R of the crest, then L, using a chimney, narrowing towards the top. From here an easy scramble leads to the summit (about $2\frac{1}{2}$ h. from hut).

<u>Egginergrat (Egginer-Mittaghorn Ridge)</u>. A fine traverse on excellent gneiss, long, with a variety of problems and many short variations to particular pitches. It is always best to traverse the gendarmes, although some can be turned more easily by looser rock on the flanks. AD, pitches of III/III+. In case of bad weather the ridge can be left easily just below pt. 3189m., where the small Ritz glacier reaches the crest on the N side. First traverse: H. Seymour King with Ambros Supersaxo, 1883.

75. From the Mittaghorn (q. v.) follow the crest and if desired avoid obstacles on the L(E) side. Numerous bits of III. Reach a big gendarme (c. 3160m.), which is higher than the Mittaghorn, and either traverse it (III+) or turn on the L. The gap on the other side is the lowest point (3093m.) in the ridge. The climbing is now easier and the Ritz glacier rises towards the ridge from the R. Some distance further reach a large gendarme (3189m.), just above the head of the glacier; traverse it. Continue to the summit tower which has a formidable appearance. Climb direct till one is forced L along a series of ledges, to a large chimney. Climb the chimney, usually wet (III+), and finish a few m. from the summit (2½-3 h.).

MITTAGHORN 3143.5m.

A splendid training peak for parties based at Saas Fee; more variety than the Egginer, perhaps easier climbing, and for some conveniently placed directly above the Plattjen cableway terminus. First ascent by chamois hunters.

<u>East Flank</u>. The easiest route, F.

76. From the Plattjen cableway follow the approach route (48) to the Britannia hut, to below the E side of the mtn. Just after pt. 2624m., where the path descends a little, a track forks R and zigzags steeply up grass and scree to broken rocks below the summit. Climb these directly to the top (2½ h. from cableway).

<u>North-East Ridge</u>. A direct way to the top, pleasant scrambling PD-.

77. As for the previous route to the foot of the ridge (c. 2620m., large cairn and snow patch). Climb straight up scree and easy rocks to the ridge. In the lower part the crest is broken and ill defined by lying in the same plane as the N flank. Climb straight up to the summit, keeping L when in doubt (2½ h. from cableway).

<u>North-West Ridge</u>. A continuously interesting scramble on good rock, II. Recommended as the approach for traversing the Egginergrat (Route 75).

78. From Saas Fee follow the footpath to Galenalp (2054m.); here fork R along the path to the Egginerjoch with the Felskinn cableway overhead. At 2332m. a small track zigzags L up grass and scree to the foot of the ridge. Start immediately R

of and just below pt. 2686.7m. Climb straight up the crest with increasing interest and some nice pitches in the upper section to the summit (3½ h. from village).

ALPHUBELJOCH 3782m.

Between the Alphubel and Feechopf. Nowadays the quickest glacier pass from Saas to Zermatt, from the Längfluh hotel to the Täsch hut. Even finer glacier scenery than the Allalinpass, a beaten trail in summer. Both sides, F+. First tourist crossing: F.F. Tuckett and C.H. Fox with V. Tairraz and J.J. Bennen, 13 June, 1861. Reached on ski by A. von Martin and H. Rumpelt with O. Supersaxo, 29 March 1910.

79. Saas side. From the Längfluh cableway terminus the route is accurately indicated on LK, up the glacier to the S. Follow a small track which leads out on to the glacier and climb in its trough, quite close to the rock barrier on the R. At 3300m. the glacier forms a narrower raised band, and this is usually cut by large crevasses; make detours as necessary. Above 3600m. the slopes are gentle and easy and lead without incident to the broad saddle (2½ h. in ascent, 1½ h. in descent).

80. Zermatt side. From the Täsch hut take the traverse path to the SE and cross three small streams before coming to an indistinct fork to the L. Follow the latter (small track) to the E, climbing comfortable stony ground in the shallow cwm of Chummibodmen, to reach the edge of the Alphubel glacier some 200m. N of pt. 3257m. Climb the easy glacier towards a central rock rib. When close to this slant more to the R (SE), passing below an ice barrier continuation of the rib. Turn this at its far R end and finish up a steep snow slope with a few crevasses to the N. The col is a short distance to the E, at the head of a little snow cwm (3 h. in ascent, 1½ h. in descent). A variation on the glacier, under the Rotgrat wall, is sometimes quicker but it is usually hindered by large crevasses.

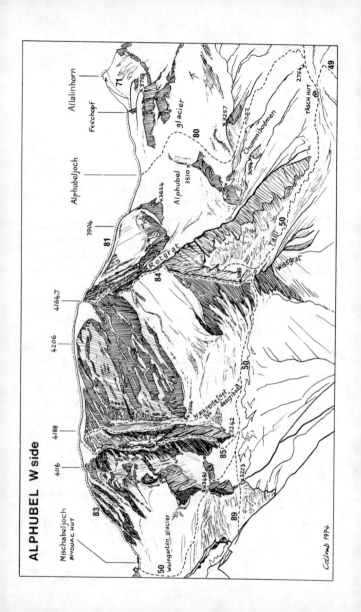

ALPHUBEL W side

PART IV

Mischabel chain

Alphubeljoch - Mischabel

ALPHUBEL 4206m.

The flat humpy summit of this mtn. is a distinctive feature of the Mischabel chain. On the summit plateau, it is almost impossible to identify the highest point in poor visibility, and when leaving the summit care should be taken to find the correct way down. A secondary pt. 4188m. is formed near the N end of the summit plateau, and there are other spot heights at the lower edges of the plateau to assist with orientation. The snowy appearance of the mtn. on the Saas side contrasts with mainly bare rockfaces on the Zermatt side. The rock is generally quite good (gneiss). All the ridges are good of their kind, but not outstanding. The Rotgrat (W) is easily the most popular; the SE ridge is generally used for descent. The less frequented N ridge and the technical W face routes are becoming more popular with the ever mounting interest shown by everyone in this mtn., but especially by parties based at Zermatt.

First ascent: Leslie Stephen and T. W. Hinchliff with Melchoir Anderegg and P. Perren, 9 August, 1860. First winter and ski ascent: A. von Martin and H. Rumpelt with O. Supersaxo, 29 March, 1910.

South-East Ridge. Generally used for descent; equally good for ascent and used as such by Saas parties. PD. First ascensionists.

81 Reach the Alphubeljoch from the Längfluh hotel or from the Täsch hut by the two previous routes ($2\frac{1}{2}$ h. or 3 h. respectively).

From the Alphubeljoch climb the pleasant snow ridge, rarely corniced, over or round pt. 3904m., to where the angle steepens and a rock band almost girdles the ridge. Here the snow covering is generally thin and the slope formed on the R can be icy (45°). If this section is in bad condition, according to the amount of snow, you can consider moving L and climbing rocks (harder), following the line of the ridge (generally delicate), or moving R and climbing the snowy rock band itself. Above, the slope eases off and you reach the highest point in 15 min. ($1\frac{1}{2}$ h. on average on col, 1 h. in descent; 4 h. from Längfluh hotel, $4\frac{1}{2}$ h. from Täsch hut).

East Flank. The shortest route on the Saas side. Entirely snow, it is particularly good for descent, giving long glissades.

A bad route for finding the way in misty weather. F+. First ascent, before 1882.

82. From the Langfluh hotel follow Route 79 to above the badly crevassed section at c. 3600m. Now slant R(W) and climb monotonous snow slopes close to a parallel rock band on your R. Cross a bergschrund and climb a very steep snow cwm direct to the summit plateau (4 h. from Längfluh hotel).

North Ridge. The shortest and probably still the least known ridge of the mtn. Above the Mischabeljoch it rises at a regular angle of about 35° with a few steeper bits for 270m. to pt. 4128m. at the NE extremity of the summit plateau. Rocks and snow. It is quite narrow and one generally climbs on the crest or a few m. down on the E side. The ridge is invariably descended in making a traverse of the mtn. PD. First ascent: W. A. B. Coolidge with Christian Almer father and son; and F. T. Wethered, F. Gardiner and M. Courtenay with P. and H. Knubel, 27 July, 1876.

83. From the Mischabeljoch (hut) keep below the rock tooth crest on the W side for 100m., then cross a small bergschrund and climb a short snow/ice slope to a small gap above the lower section of the ridge. Continue up the L side of the ridge, close to the crest, on snow, ice and rocks, and in the last third climb on the crest to the summit plateau (1 h.). Bear SW then S and reach the highest point (15 min., $1\frac{1}{4}$ h. from Mischabeljoch, 45 min. in descent).

West Ridge (Rotgrat). The longest and best known ridge of the mtn. One of the most frequented climbs in the Zermatt area and a traditional expedition for British parties. Mainly rocky with a longish intermediate snow shoulder. The lower part splits into two branches, and the more northerly arm is called the Wissgrat. The rock is somewhat loose at the most delicate point on the climb, in the upper couloir, where stonefall is also possible. PD. First ascent: George Broke with X. and A. Andenmattern, 1889.

84. From the Täsch hut follow Route 50 to the stone circle of cairns (c. 3140m.) in the Tälli cwm, beside the Wissgrat arm of the ridge (1¼ h.). Now climb along the Wissgrat, over scree, easy rocks and scree covered slabs, either on the crest or slightly L of it, up to the rock knoll pt. 3637m., where the two branches of the ridge join. Reach the snow above by turning the knoll on the L by loose slabs.

Alternatively, it is more interesting to continue into the Tälli cwm and reach the crest of the Wissgrat by climbing up its side wall where the rocks between the cwm bed and the crest are lowest, about half-way along to pt. 3637m. The side gives two or three short pitches of II on scratched rocks (1½ h.).

Climb along the broad crest of the intermediate snow shoulder to a flat section at its top (45 min.). The rocks above are very steep, so make a rising traverse R along a gangway system to a couloir in the S flank of the ridge. The couloir is steep; climb rocks on either side - the L-hand side being more usual, with some loose blocks, and rejoin the crest by moving R. This section is quite delicate when snow covered or icy. Now follow the crest to where the ridge reaches the summit plateau (4164.7m.). Turn L(N) and reach the summit in 300m. (2¼ h., 5¾ h. from Täsch hut).

West Ridge of North Summit. This flying buttress is perfectly defined. It has a clean cut toe (3242m.) and finishes close to pt. 4116m. at the NW edge of the summit plateau (this point actually marks the top of the ill defined WNW ridge). The rock is gneiss and does not lie in the same inhospitable strata which characterise the the W face of the mtn. further R. One of the best rock climbs of its standard in the Mischabel chain. Competent Britist climbers will find the climbing of ordinary "V.

Diff^r. standard with a few harder moves. AD+, pitches of III/ III+ and the crux, IV+. 900m. First ascent: E. Wyss-Dunant with A. Lerjen and P. Mooser, 27 July, 1945. First British (third) ascent: J.T.H. Allen, J.W. Gatiss and G.F. Dixon, 6 August, 1956. Now climbed frequently.

85. From the Täsch hut follow Route 50 to the foot of the ridge (2 h.). Go round the foot to the L, on snow, and climb the first rake line in this flank to reach the crest (II, 30 min.). Follow the crest and climb a succession of slabs and short walls direct for 250m. with some loose rock (III-) to a tower (3615m.), which is traversed (III+) to a small snowy gap. An easier section on broken rock of 150m. leads to a sharp gendarme. Make a slightly descending traverse R on doubtful flakes into a corner. Climb round to the R and up to a small niche in a steep wall. Take an exposed crack up this wall to rejoin the crest (IV- for 10m.). Easy blocks on the ridge lead to a fine crest, then to a series of steep slabs curling over to the L. Climb these with increasing difficulty, keeping to the R-hand side. Near the top of this section reach the base of a smooth slab pitch. From its R side (exposed drop) climb direct and with difficulty for a few m. (IV+) and continue to a large pulpit (30m.). Now trend R over broken rock towards a rock couloir which has a pronounced narrow rib on the far side. Climb short walls and slabs straight up between the ridge and the couloir, then cross the head of the couloir to finish up a series of pleasant cracks at the summit plateau. Alternatively, in good conditions, rocks in the bed of the couloir will be found easier (6-7 h., $8\frac{1}{2}$-$9\frac{1}{2}$ h. from Täsch hut).

MISCHABELJOCH 3851m.

Between the Alphubel and Täschhorn, one of the finest cols in the Pennine Alps, with a small hut on the first rocks of the Täschhorn. See Routes 50 and 51. Rarely used as a crossing

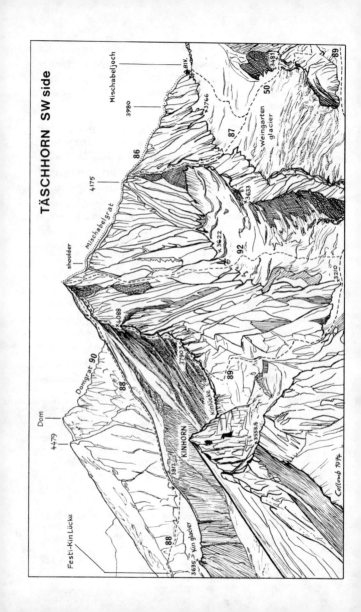

TÄSCHHORN SW side

Festi-Kin Lücke

Dom
4479

Dom grat 90

shoulder

Mischabelgrat

4175

86

87

Mischabeljoch

3980

×3766

BIV.

3491

50

weingarten
glacier

88

88

88

×088

3812

3790

3635 › Kin glacier

KINHORN

Kinlücke

89

89

92

×3622

3633

3310

3558.8

Collomb 1974

89

from Saas to Zermatt because it is higher and more difficult than the Alphubeljoch and Allalinpass. Both sides are climbed fairly often now because the bivouac hut has greatly facilitated the ascent of the Täschhorn.

First traverse: H. B. George, Coutts Trotter, W. Trotter and W. S. Thomason with C. Almer, P. Bohren and F. Andenmatten, 30 July, 1862.

TÄSCHHORN 4490.7m.

In partnership with its taller neighbour the Dom, this magnificent peak forms the apogee of the Mischabel chain proper. Superior in every way to the Dom except altitude, it is one of the most sought after summits in the whole of the Alps, and is one of the two or three most difficult 4000m. peaks described in this guide. In the Zermatt district only the Dent d'Hérens is a more serious proposition.

The topography is fairly simple; three great ridges, one of which links the Dom, and three huge faces. There is a certain similarity of character about the ridges, but the faces differ noticeably. The Saas (E) face is a regular snow and rock wall corrugated by rock ribs and couloirs. The Täschalp (SW) face is a formidable recessed wall. The Kin (NW) face is a broken glacier slope with no rocks at all.

Before the construction of the hut on the Mischabeljoch, the mtn. was rarely climbed from Saas. Because of its relative difficulty it is one of the least frequented of the Zermatt host peaks; about 50 ascents per annum at present, but the new hut is attracting more parties, both from Saas and Zermatt, to the mtn. every year.

In good conditions the technical difficulty of the ordinary routes is not of a high order. One can rarely find a pitch of II. Snow and ice problems are always more serious. The length of the climbs, combined with mixed terrain, extremely variable conditions and great altitude, demand all-round competence and fitness. The most serious aspect of climbing the Täschhorn is that if caught in a storm there is no easy way down. On the whole the rocks are friable, but some are good; one meets both kinds alternately on any given route.

First ascent: J. L. Davies and J. H. Hayward with J. and S. Zumtaugwald and P. J. Summermatter, 30 July, 1862. First winter and ski ascent: Marcel Kurz with J. Knubel, 7 February, 1920.

<u>South-East Ridge (Mischabelgrat)</u>. In very good conditions this ridge is entirely rocky, except at the prominent upper snow shoulder (c. 4350m.) below the summit pyramid. Crossing this

shoulder is the crux in all conditions. From the Mischabel-joch the ridge rises in regular and gradual curving sections with no outstanding obstacles. The first step above the col looks the steepest (except for the summit pyramid) and is some-times called the Grand Gendarme (3980m.). Between fairly indistinct knolls marking sections of the ridge, snow crests are likely to form, especially in the lower half of the climb between the top of the Grand Gendarme and the upper shoulder. The junction of the W rib variation and the main ridge at pt. 4175m. is not at all evident. In good conditions the rocks of the final pyramid are easy and fresh snow clears quickly.

On the whole this ridge is the easiest way up the mtn. While the vertical interval between the Mischabeljoch and the summit is only 650m., the ridge is long, and it is narrow enough to make rapid progress difficult except in perfect conditions. The climb is hard to compare with the NW face (Dom hut route), which can be absolutely straightforward in crampons and good snow. PD+, delicate, a magnificent expedition with splendid situations and remarkable views. If the correct route is fol-lowed there is only 3m. of II along the entire ridge.

First ascent: J. Jackson with C. and U. Almer, 15 August, 1876.

86. From the Mischabeljoch climb broken rocks on the R of the crest, first up an open chimney, then in a staircase formation to a break halfway up the first step. Climb on the broad crest, then move L and zigzag up a section of bad rock, at the top of which you cross to the R. Reach the top of the step without dif-ficulty, descend a few m., then turn the next low tower by an horizontal traverse to the R. Cross a rib coming down from the top of this tower (about 15m. above) by climbing R across a nice little slab (3m., II). On the other side climb down on the crest and continue over the next rocky knolls to the first snow crest. There are usually four of these, all short, sep-arated by easy rock steps. Climb precisely on the crest everywhere, with occasional movements to the L to avoid unnecessary difficulties. Cross the knoll (4175m.) at the junction with the W rib and continue over two more knolls, the second of which is short and steep (turn on R a few m. below its top). Reach a snow and rock section, very steep, which is best climbed on the edge (25m.). Easy work on the crest, always narrow, leads to short and sometimes corniced snow crests, and finally to a big snow hump forming the lower end of the upper shoulder ($2\frac{3}{4}$ h.). In good conditions a steep rock platform is exposed along the base of the shoulder on its L side, overlooking the SW face. This ledge (delicate) can be followed to below the highest point of the shoulder, which is then reached with crampons or step cutting by a direct ascent. Huge cornice possible on other side! It is more usual to climb on the crest of the shoulder from its lower end and follow the narrow crest to the horizontal section which connects it to the summit pyramid. If the cornice on the R is large, you must make a slightly descending traverse L on very steep snow or ice (delicate, two rope lengths) (30 min.). Above the shoulder climb snowy rocks on the R side of a vague couloir to reach more continuous rocks. Climb these straight up, then trend R along a break line to a crest of red rocks. Climb the crest pleasantly to finish a few m. R of the summit (45 min., about 4 h. from Mischabeljoch, 3 h. in descent).

87. Variation. If starting from the Täsch hut it is not necessary to reach the Mischabeljoch first of all. Follow Route 50 to above the icefall complex on the Weingarten glacier and continue up the L side towards the Mischabeljoch, to c. 3620m. On your L is the W rib rising to the main ridge at pt. 4175m. Climb the side of the rib by crossing the bergschrund and taking a rib of broken rocks on the L of a narrow snow couloir, which goes up to a little saddle in the W rib at c. 3750m. PD+ ($3\frac{1}{2}$ h. from hut). From this saddle climb the broad rib of snowy rocks, with snow grooves and scree, to pt. 4175m. ($1\frac{1}{4}$ h.). Then as

for the previous Route to the summit ($2\frac{3}{4}$ h., about $7\frac{1}{2}$ h. from Täsch hut).

North-West (Kin) Face. One of the best climbs of its standard on snow or ice in the Zermatt region, comparable with the WNW face of the Dent d'Hérens. In conditions of good snow throughout it can be counted as the easiest way up the mtn. The normal route from the Dom hut. If the face is predominantly icy it is probably not worth trying because of the time you will lose in step cutting. In the last 20 years this route has been climbed more often than the Mischabelgrat, but this situation is likely to alter with the appearance of a hut at the foot of the latter ridge. Many years ago the face was reached directly up the Kin glacier, the lower part of which is now riddled with crevasses (and the approach path below that has become a vertical jungle through disuse). One reaches the upper plateau of the Kin glacier by crossing the Festi-Kin Lücke (3734m.), a saddle about 100m. E of the snow cap marked pt. 3768m. Reaching this saddle is one of the two main problems of the climb. The steepest part of the face itself is halfway up, where a large bergschrund and surrounding ice walls guard the head of its lower constricted portion. A rope of three is best. PD+/AD.

First ascensionists, by the Kin glacier approach. The modern approach (described below) was first used in descent by Oscar Hug with S. Burgener, August, 1915.

88. From the Dom hut follow Route 95 till you are beside the rock buttress just above pt. 3303m. on the L side of the Festi glacier, above its crevassed zone ($1\frac{1}{4}$ h.). Start crossing the glacier to the R and bear SE into a snow cwm below the ridge dividing the Festi and Kin glaciers. Go up the snow cwm, approaching the R side of the glacier all the while. After passing below pt. 3768m. move R to the bergschrund under the steep snow/ice wall of the Festi-Kin Lücke. This is the lowest

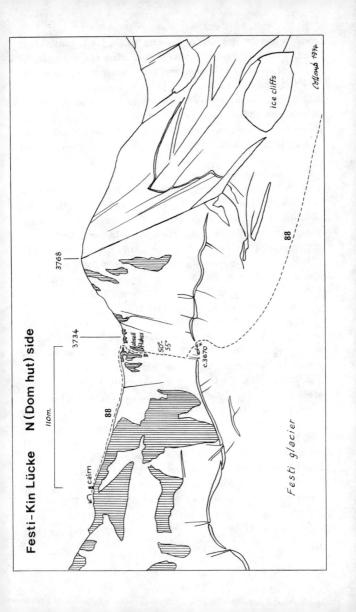

Festi-Kin Lücke N (Dom hut) side

3768

3734

110m.

a cairn

88

88

88

50°-55°

fossil B flakes

c.3670

ice cliffs

Festi glacier

Colomb 1974

point in this section of the dividing ridge.   Alternatively, if
the traverse movement across the glacier from above pt. 3303m.
is complicated by crevasses (there are an increasing number in
this flat section of the glacier), continue towards the Festijoch
(Route 95), and on arriving below that col, traverse the glacier
at c. 3600m. There is an intermediate glacier rib, badly crevassed at its base, so climb up its N flank for 50m. before continuing to the S.   This variation is about 15 min. longer than
the usual way.

  Cross the bergschrund below the col (sometimes very large),
move L for a few m. then climb the snow/ice wall direct to the
lowest rocks (40-50m., 55°).   There is a big rock flake with
old slings on it (abseil in descent). Now climb flaky rocks and
steep snow to the ridge, slightly L of the lowest point (25m.).
If this section is ice, a lot of step cutting may be necessary.
Climb along the broad and easy rock ridge to the E for 110m.
Reach a large cairn. Do not attempt to descend from the ridge
before this point (i.e. you do not descend from the point of
arrival above the snow/ice wall) ($1\frac{1}{2}$ h.).

  A few m. higher up from the cairn, make a descending traverse down the other side of the ridge towards the Kin glacier,
very steep but easy rocks at the top, easing lower down. Cross
a shallow gritty couloir before reaching the bottom at c. 3720m.
The loss of height is about 100m. Go up the L side of the Kin
glacier, almost flat, for a short way, then traverse it to the S,
turning a little to the SW in order to reach the crest of the
glacier spur coming down the narrows at the foot of the NW
face (a few crevasses).   Climb along the back of the spur and
continue straight up a plain snow slope towards a large bergschrund and complex of ice walls ($1\frac{1}{4}$ h.).   Cross the bergschrund on the R (it can be wide and very difficult), and make
a rising traverse up a steep snow/ice wall to the R. This movement leads away from all difficulties, but the slope is up to
55° for the first 50m., easing off as one gets higher. Continue

making a rising traverse to the R to within 100m. or less of the Teufelsgrat. Now trend L below a small bergschrund and climb parallel with and below the ridge till near the last small step in the Teufelsgrat. Climb towards the step (the bergschrund has usually disappeared at this point), turn the foot of it on the L and climb steep snow in a sort of couloir behind it up to the ridge (1 h.). The ridge can be very icy (many parties turned back from a point as high as this) but its rocks are otherwise not difficult. Climb on the flaky crest, or just below it on the L (30-45 min., about $5\frac{3}{4}$-6 h. from Dom hut). With good snow and crampons this route is very quick in descent.

West-South-West Ridge (Teufelsgrat). No other climb in the Zermatt district has been surrounded with so much awe and mystery as this one; or has had its difficulties so exaggerated. It is the longest ridge on the mtn. , the starting points are distant from where the real climbing begins and the rock is bad. In good conditions the serious part of the ridge is almost entirely rocky, but there are delicate bits on snow or ice. Several pitches of III and borderline IV on good and bad rock. It is always better to stay on the crest where the rocks are more difficult than to turn steep pitches on much worse rock on the flanks. Not a particularly good climb (aptly described by R. R. E. Chorley as a "flat" ridge), but aesthetically interesting. AD+. First ascent: A. F. Mummery and Mrs. M. Mummery with Alexander Burgener and another guide, 16 July, 1887. First winter ascent: G. Gnos, A. Herger and G. Bumann, 20 March, 1973.

89. From the Täsch hut follow Route 50 to below pt. 3242m., then traverse L(N) and pass below the foot (c. 3240m.) of the rock wall under the central section of the Weingarten glacier. Now cross this glacier at c. 3180m., generally a maze of crevasses, and at the same level cross the opening to the N branch of the glacier, arriving at its N bank near pt. 3210m. ($2\frac{3}{4}$ h.).

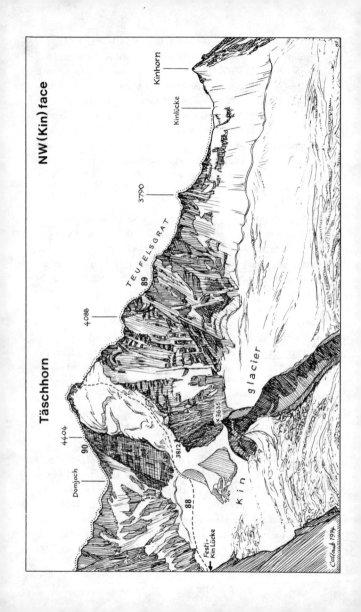

Above is a couloir coming down from a gap to the R of the Kinhorn (3752m.). Go up scree into the couloir, climb it for 20m., then traverse out using ledges rising to the R. These lead to easy slabs topped by a short vertical chimney in a zone of wet yellow rocks. Climb the chimney and continue rising R over slabs, scree and snow beds to reach the main ridge at the foot of the first gendarme/step (3790m.) (2 h.).

Climb this first step by its crest (III). A short descent to a gap is followed by a sharp rock crest, often snowy, leading to a foot of a steeper step. The approach to this step is formed by flaky rocks, with good holds, which can be mounted with a leg on either side. The step above (c. 3890m.) is less difficult than it looks. Climb the crest to a vertical bit which can be overcome by taking a shoulder. An easier section follows to another vertical riser. Traverse R along a narrow ledge of rotten rock and regain the crest at a small snow saddle above the top of the step and below the largest tower (4088m.). Climb straight up its crest (III+/IV) to the top and make a short descent to a gap. The ridge steepens again and is broader. Climb the crest to the foot of a vertical riser. Traverse L along a ledge line, then make a rising traverse across the N flank to an icy black chimney. Climb this (25m., III+/IV) to the crest above the top of the tower. Continue along the crest to a narrow gap. Climb directly into it (10m., good rock) and out again by a rock staircase to where the ridge eases off and becomes snowy (about 4 h.). Climb an easy snow slope on the L and join Route 88 below the last step in the ridge, which can be turned on the L (1 h., about $9\frac{3}{4}$ h. from Täsch hut).

Täschhorn-Dom Ridge (Domgrat). The Domgrat is invariably traversed in the direction Täschhorn-Dom, so that there is an easy descent at the far end. The traverse of both mtns. by this ridge, which is in a superb position above the Saas valley, is one of the finest expeditions in the Pennine Alps. From the

Täschhorn the ridge falls regularly to its lowest point, the Dom-joch (4281m.), and from there rises to the Dom with similar regularity but in more pronounced steps. In ideal but rarely seen conditions the ridge is mainly rocky with pitches of II/II+ maximum. Such conditions are unusual, such as when parties have done the ridge in $1\frac{1}{2}$ h. Normally the ridge carries a fair amount of snow, in keeping with its great altitude. The rocks verglas easily and the ridge quickly becomes difficult. Conditions vary tremendously. PD/AD+ or harder. First traverse in this direction: O. G. Jones with Elias Furrer, 3 September, 1895. Probably two parties had done the ridge in the reverse direction the year before.

90. From the Täschhorn follow the mainly snowy ridge, broad, to a narrowing where it drops over a forepeak. Climb down rocks and continue along the crest, delicate, to a rock knoll (4404m.); climb down this on or near the crest (II) and reach a more continuously rocky section of the ridge, usually mixed with snow. Follow it to the snowy Domjoch saddle; cornices on L (1 h.). The corniced ridge with a few rocks leads to a gendarme. Climb over it (II+) or turn on the R(E), the latter on unpleasantly loose but easy rock. The ridge is now mainly rocky with a number of teeth and gaps. These can be climbed or turned on the R, according to conditions. Some of the rock is poor. In bad conditions the gaps are filled with delicate snow crests. At the end of this section arrive at an almost horizontal shoulder running against a buttress below the summit of the Dom. Climb this terminal buttress direct (II+), good rock, and finish on snowy rocks a few m. below the summit ($2\frac{1}{2}$ h., $3\frac{1}{2}$ h. on average from Täschhorn).

91. <u>East Face</u>. The Saas side of the Täschhorn and Dom has been climbed at various points. The faces of both mtns. are seamed by couloirs and ribs, generally well covered with snow, and throughout their length at all points are seriously exposed

134

to stonefall and avalanches. The rock is also poor. A direct line to the Täschhorn summit was achieved a century ago by a powerful team of the day (F.T. Wethered and P. Watson with Alexander Burgener, B. Venetz and L. Proment, 6 August, 1876). Technically not a serious route but unpleasant and dangerous. AD+, 700m. plus a complicated and often difficult glacier approach from the Längfluh hotel. It has seldom been repeated. and these remarks apply to all other routes and variations on this side.

92. <u>South-West Face</u>. This tremendous rock wall is nearly 900m. high above the toe of its lowest rock rib (3622m.). While the technical difficulties are not excessive, the route is rated as one of the most unusual rock climbs on a big mtn. anywhere in the Alps. The face has been likened to a near-vertical slag heap, held together well or badly by a wide range of possible temperatures and variable amounts of snow or ice welding the joints. The face is ordinarily swept by stonefall and successful parties have chosen near ideal conditions to minimise the danger. The rib is climbed more or less directly to a huge diédre on the R in the upper part of the face, finishing on the Mischabelgrat about 15m. below the summit. An extremely cold night and morning, and the rocks free from snow and ice, are essential conditions for safety. Times from the foot of the face have varied from 8 to 15 h. TD+. First ascent: V.J.E. Ryan with F. and J. Lochmatter; and G.W. Young with Josef Knubel, 11 August, 1906. Climbed about a dozen times to date. First winter ascent: U. Hürlimann and A. Strickler, 23 February, 1964.

KINHORN 3752m.

A sharp little peak, hardly ever climbed. Its E foot is reached by the approach to the Teufelsgrat. By the main ridge from

E side

Dom

Lenzjoch

Lenzspitze

105

Nadel

100

100

101

Dreieselwand

Hohbalm glacier

MISCHABEL HUT

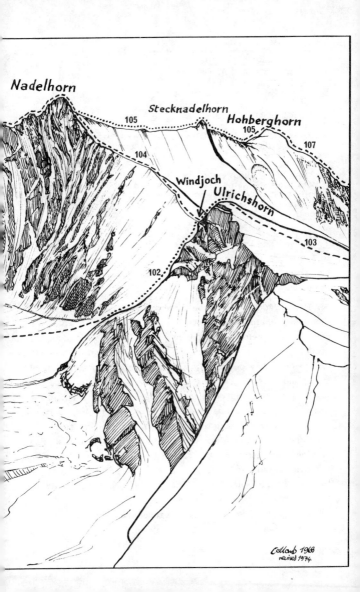

Nadelhorn

Stecknadelhorn

Hohberghorn

105

105

107

104

Windjoch

Ulrichshorn

103

102

Collomb 1968
revised 1974

here, across the Kinlücke gap, a short rock climb of II+. First ascent (by NNW ridge): W. E. Utterson-Kelso, C. J. Ord, F. Baylis and two ladies, with A. and X. Andenmatten, J. M. Blumental and A. Gentinetta, 25 July, 1883.

LEITERSPITZEN 3409m.

A useful rock climb for training purposes, or when the high peaks are out of condition. Slow parties unaccustomed to moving quickly on fairly difficult rock have been known to take up to 15 h. to traverse the mtn. The summit is formed by twin rock thumbs at the E end of the fine W ridge. The more easterly of the two thumbs is not usually climbed. The rock is excellent and the hardest pitches still bristle with old stanchions and pegs which formerly held fixed ropes. First ascent not traced.

Traverse. The ordinary way of climbing the mtn. and a practical way for starting and finishing at the Täschalp inn, the only convenient starting point. Pitches of III and IV, fairly sustained and pleasantly exposed.

93. From Täschalp inn descend the metalled road for a few m. then take a mule path to the R and cross the stream. This path contours NW below a rock barrier and is followed for a few min. till the barrier peters out above. Just before the path crosses a wide stone chute, turn R and climb rough slopes of grass and rock (vague track) to a shoulder. From here you can see a ravine coming down from a little col at the L end of the W ridge. On its immediate L is the peaklet 3214m. (Alternatively, after crossing the bridge over the stream, turn R at once and follow a small path near the R bank of the stream coming down from the Weingarten glacier. After some steep zigzags the path leads L across a high grassy shelf well above the rock barrier mentioned previously; so reach the shoulder. This approach is less tiring but longer).

From the shoulder climb NE over scree and easy rocks, keeping the ravine on your L all the way up. Finally some steep slabs closer to the ravine are climbed, bearing E, to reach the col (c. 3170m.) (2 h.).

On the crest of the ridge climb nice slab pitches (II/II+) to the first big gendarme. Take a slabby wall on the L (II+) to its summit and descend the crest to a gap. Above is a steep step. Ascend direct, using pegs in place (IV), and belay on a stanchion near the top (3268m.). A number of lesser steps and gaps lead to a tower and another gap (II and III). Above this gap is a sheer gendarme, pierced by a hole, and with two cracks in its wall. Climb the L-hand crack (IV), traverse L and finish up a fine slab (III+) to the top of the gendarme. A razor edge (III) with a drop of 8m. in it at one point (abseil) leads to the summit cairn (3 h., 5 h. from Täschalp inn).

94. Descent: From the summit cairn descend the crest of the SSW ridge on your R for 15m. (steep, II+, abseil if required), followed by an easier 20m. to a large fixed peg. From here make a vertical 12m. abseil down the W(R-hand) side of the ridge to land on small ledges. Go L along a narrow ledge rising at 40° to a nick. From here descend a steep slanting crack and groove line into a couloir which is followed to scree below. Cross rough slopes SW and go over a scree saddle just N of the shoulder pt. 3051m. Further down reach the approach route and so return to the inn. (Alternatively, from the bottom of the gully carry on straight down a steep grassy rib which bounds the gully. Find an intermittent track which descends to the big track by the stream at the bottom) (3 h. for descent).

DOMJOCH 4281m.

The lowest point in the ridge (Domgrat) between the Täschhorn and Dom. See Route 90. While only about PD standard on the Zermatt side, the Saas side is steep and unpleasant. Not used as a pass and rarely done on the W side except as an emergency descent from the Domgrat. Traversed by G. E. Foster and H. Walker with J. Anderegg and H. Baumann, 20 July, 1869.

DOM 4545.4m.

The crowning point of the Mischabel and the highest mtn. situated entirely in Switzerland. Its structure is more complex than the companion Täschhorn, with which it does not compare favourably for climbing interest. The ascent is quite easy. Needless to say it is one of the most popular outings in the Zermatt district. The mtn. is rarely climbed from Saas Fee.

For the classic traverse of the Täschhorn and Dom, either reach the former from the Mischabeljoch hut by Route 86, or from the Dom hut by Route 88, follow the Domgrat to its summit (Route 90), and descend by Route 95 to the Dom hut (12-16 h. according to route and conditions).

First ascent: J. L. Davies with J. Zumtaugwald, J. Kronig and H. Brantschen, 11 September, 1858. First winter ascent: Sydney Spencer with C. Jossi and A. Schaller, 13 January, 1894. First ski ascent: Arnold Lunn with J. Knubel, 18 June, 1917. All three ascents in their turn were the cause of some celebration in the Zermatt valley.

North Flank. The normal and easiest route, something of a snow trudge. With care you can make a very long glissade from near the summit to the Hohberg glacier at the bottom of the N flank. F+. First ascent not traced.

95. From the Dom hut a steep track goes ESE up moraine on the L side of the Festi glacier to a shoulder where the lateral moraine crest starts. Follow this to large blocks which are crossed in the same direction to reach snowbeds beside the glacier (1 h.). Start up the L side of the glacier, turn a promontory above pt. 3303m. and continue into a shallow cwm (crevasses) and the upper snowfields. Keep close to the rock wall on your L and continue for some distance to below the Festijoch (3723m.). The col is marked by a large "signal" on a higher point to its L. On the R the ridge above it rises steeply towards the Dom. Climb loose rocks and scree, slanting R, to the col (traces of a path) (1½ h.). On the other side a short steep snow/

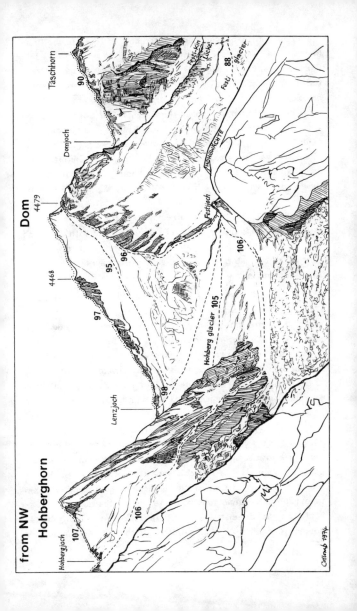

ice slope with a bergschrund at the bottom leads to the Hohberg glacier (20m.). Cross the flat glacier towards the Nadelhorn and pass below an icefall (séracs) on your R. Debris from falling ice often litters tracks on the glacier, so this point should be crossed quickly! Gradually work R (crevasses) towards the Lenzjoch, rising to the foot of the snowy N flank of the Dom on your R. Climb the big slope trending R, and in the upper part bear L to reach a snow saddle above the steep part of the NW ridge, between the gendarme pt. 4479m. and the summit. Now climb an easy snow ridge to the highest point, narrow and sometimes corniced ($3\frac{1}{2}$ h., 6 h. from Dom hut; $3\frac{1}{4}$ h. in descent).

North-West Ridge. A more direct way up the mtn. The ridge is fairly broad, partly slabby and often plastered with snow and ice. It is best climbed in crampons throughout. Not very interesting, somewhat more sporting than the usual way. PD-. First ascensionists.

96. From the Dom hut reach the Festijoch by the previous route ($2\frac{1}{2}$ h.). Climb straight up the rocky ridge, formed by rounded slabs which are smooth but easy. When the snow is good more rapid progress can be made by keeping L in long snow grooves. Higher up the crest is often icy, so keep L between it and séracs further L. Return to the crest when convenient. At the top of the ridge turn a gendarme (4479m.) by snow on its L and join the previous route just below the summit (3 h., $5\frac{1}{2}$ h. from Dom hut).

97. **North-East Ridge.** The main ridge rising from the Lenzjoch. Its lower and upper sections are easy, but the middle part is occupied by a difficult serrated rock crest which culminates in a Grand Gendarme (4468m.). Unfortunately this topographically important ridge is one of the most pointless routes in the Zermatt region. It is flanked artificially by the normal N side route; the climbing is too remote and neither

142

good enough nor on good enough rock to make the effort worthwhile. If the ridge was in a better position the story might be
different. D+ (3-6 h. from Lenzjoch to summit). First ascent:
U. Campell, G. Truog, A. Roch and A. Dunant, 31 July, 1928.
First British (second) ascent: C. W. F. Noyce with A. Lagger,
5 August, 1937. Probably not climbed more than 20 times.

LENZJOCH 4121m.

Between the Dom and Lenzspitze. Not used as a pass today
(quite tricky on Saas side). Approached or reached by routes on
the Lenzspitze and Dom from the Zermatt (Dom hut) side. Dis-
cussions have been held about erecting a bivouac hut on this
pass. The idea seems to have no sound justification, although
the reason advanced seems to be to safeguard slow parties finishing the Nadelgrat traverse too late to reach the Dom hut.
  First traverse: G. E. Foster and H. Walker with J. Anderegg
and H. Baumann, 16 July, 1869.

LENZSPITZE 4294m.

This fine peak loses something in appearance when seen from
the W (Dom hut) side because it forms the SE end of the Nadelgrat, which is dominated centrally by the Nadelhorn. The mtn.
asserts itself more prominently from the Saas side, and it is on
this side that it provides routes of considerable interest. A
connoisseur's peak.
  From the Zermatt (Dom hut) side the summit is more often
reached in making a traverse of the Nadelgrat, but it can be
climbed for its own sake without much difficulty. In fact the
Lenzspitze is one of the most difficult 4000m. peaks in the
region. Contrary to some recommendations concerning more
direct routes up the rocky W flank, the only completely satisfactory route from the W is the ridge rising from the Lenzjoch. The W flank is steep and loose and often delicate because
of soft snow and ice, but one line is practised quite frequently.
  First ascent: C. T. Dent with A. and F. Burgener, August,
1870. First winter and ski ascent: H. Rey and L. Gelpke with
H. Supersaxo, 25 March, 1918.

South Ridge (Lenzjoch). The best route from the Dom hut. It gives you a taste of better things to be found further along the Nadelgrat. The rocks are covered with nail scratches. Quite interesting. PD. First ascent: R. F. Ball with A. Supersaxo and L. Zurbriggen, 28 July, 1888.

98. From the Dom hut follow Route 95 to below the N flank of the Dom, then climb easily to a bergschrund below the Lenzjoch. Cross it and reach the col by a short steep snow/ice slope and a few rocks (4 h.). From the col follow the loose rock crest, delicate when snow covered, to the foot of a prominent gendarme (c. 4200m.). Turn this on the R, using broken ledges, and return to the crest at a scree saddle. Move L into a rock couloir below the crest and lying in the same plane. Climb its broken rocks to the crest again not far from the summit. Continue up a fine snow and rock crest to the summit ($1\frac{1}{2}$ h., 1 h. in descent, $5\frac{1}{2}$ h. from Dom hut).

South Ridge by West Flank Variation. This alternative to the previous route has some following, especially in descent. It is a bit loose and unpleasant when soft snow is lying on the flank. PD.

99. From the Dom hut follow the previous route to a short distance below the Lenzjoch bergschrund. Slant L(N) till you are below the prominent gendarme on the S ridge above. Cross the bergschrund and climb steep snow or ice to a broken scree and rock slope, often snowy. Slant somewhat L and reach the ridge to the L of the gendarme where the previous route is joined. It is also possible to slant R and join the ridge below the gendarme ($5\frac{1}{2}$ h. from Dom hut to summit).

East-North-East Ridge. The most direct way to the summit from the Mischabel hut, slightly more technical than anything on the Nadelgrat, which is usually followed to the Nadelhorn as a convenient means of returning to the hut. Varied climbing in a fine position on rock and ice, PD+. First ascent: W. W. Graham with A. Supersaxo and T. Andenmatten, 3 August, 1882.

100. From the Mischabel hut a small track climbs rounded rocks due W above the hut site. The track is fairly clear up to where the rock spur widens and steepens.   So reach the point (c. 3620m, 45 min.) where the route to the Windjoch moves R. Climb to the L up the main ridge, either on the crest or just L of it to avoid small obstacles, on loose easy rock, to reach pt. 3815m. (30 min.).   From here a short horizontal snow crest leads to snowy rocks and a steeper ridge.   Climb the crest as directly as possible. After a slight dip reach the foot of the Grand Gendarme (c. 4090m.).   This should be traversed by the crest (III), on reasonably good rock, hard in conditions of fresh snow. The flanks are very loose. From the top of the gendarme abseil 5m. to a near-horizontal section of the ridge which leads to a comfortable resting place ($1\frac{1}{2}$ h.).   Now climb L along a narrow rising ledge line, then in zigzags up easy but rotten rock which requires care, to the final snow/ice crest. This leads delicately to the summit;   alternatively use loose rock on the L below the crest ($1\frac{1}{4}$ h., about 4 h. from Mischabel hut).

<u>North-North-East Face (Dreieselwand)</u>. This symmetrical snow/ice wall is the most conspicuous feature of the mtn. It is the finest pure ice climb in the Mischabel chain and one of the finest of its class in the Pennine Alps, comparable with the NNE face of the Obergabelhorn. A regular slope of 50°, rather more at the top, and a straightforward exercise with crampons in good snow conditions. Otherwise much step cutting and in poor conditions very delicate. D, 490m. The 1911 party climbed the L side of the face, near rock outcrops extending from the ENE ridge and finished on this ridge. The modern direct route starts R of the summit line and slants gradually L

to finish almost at the top of the ENE ridge. Climbed frequently.

First (indirect) ascent: D. von Bethmann-Hollweg with O. and O. Supersaxo, 7 July, 1911. First direct (and solo) ascent: Hans Frei, 20 July, 1933 (in 2 h.). First British ascent: H. G. Nicol and R. Prager, 25 July, 1962. First winter ascent: P. Etter and H. Wenin. 1-2 March, 1968. Descended on ski by H. Holzer, 22 July, 1972.

101. From the Mischabel hut follow the previous route to where you can move R on to the Hohbalm glacier. Climb easily up the glacier to the foot of the face, at its R side below the depression of the Nadeljoch in the ridge above. From this point a direct line to the summit slants L (1½ h.). Cross the bergschrund (3800m.) and climb the plain slope to the top. It is usual to finish somewhat L of the summit, on the ENE ridge (4-6 h., about 6½ h. on average from hut).

<u>North-West Ridge</u>. The main ridge of the mtn., coming from the Nadelhorn. The lowest point between the two is called the Nadeljoch (4213m.*). This ridge forms part of the Nadelgrat traverse which is described in Route 105. First ascensionists.

NADELHORN 4327m.

In itself not a very important mtn., but it forms the centrepiece of the Nadelgrat, and its ridge provides the best rock climbing found on this traverse. Whereas the ridge is composed of excellent gneiss, the flanks are loose and the rocks discontinuous. A short distance below the cairn, the summit is pierced by a conspicuous hole. The mtn. is climbed for itself fairly often from the Mischabel hut; less frequently as such from the Dom hut because one traverses it as part of the Nadelgrat (Route 105). The most popular combination from the Mischabel hut is to climb the Lenzspitze by Route 100, reverse the Nadelgrat section (Route 105) to the Nadelhorn, and return to the hut by Route 102.

First ascent: J. Zimmermann, A. Supersaxo, B. Epiney and F. Andenmatten, 16 September, 1858. First winter and ski ascent: H. Rey and L. Gelpke, 25 March 1918.

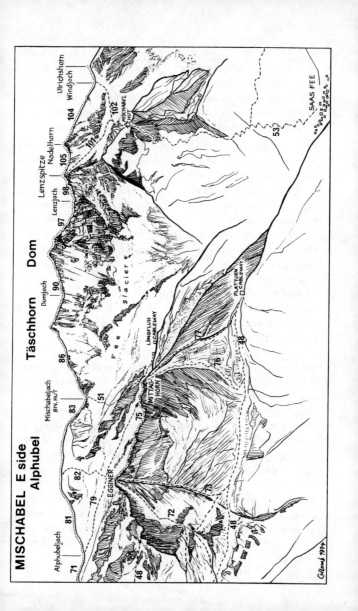

North-East Ridge (Windjoch and Ulrichshorn). The ordinary route from the Mischabel hut and the easiest way up or down the mtn. A popular climb, varied and interesting. The upper rocks are often icy, so it is usual to seek an advantage in climbing continuous snow strips near the crest. In good conditions the route is very quick in descent. PD-. First ascensionists.

102. From the Mischabel hut a small track climbs rounded rocks due W above the hut site. The track is fairly clear up to where the rocky spur widens and steepens. So reach the point (c. 3620m.) (45 min.) where you can walk R and descend slightly to the Hohbalm glacier. Cross the glacier by making a circling movement W and N to reach the foot of the Windjoch (3850m.). Climb the steep snow slope above, trending R towards the Ulrichshorn, and at mid-height slant back L and in a rising traverse reach the col (45 min., $1\frac{1}{2}$ h. from hut. 45 min. in descent).

From the Windjoch you can climb the fine SW snow ridge of the Ulrichshorn (3925m.) in 30 min. or less. This ridge is rarely corniced but is narrow and sometimes icy. The summit is frequently visited while climbing the Nadelhorn.

103. If you start from the Bordier hut to reach the Windjoch, the final slope above the Ried glacier is steep and normally icy. It is better to traverse the Ulrichshorn to reach the col. The route from the Bordier hut up the L side of the Ried glacier is easy to find but crevassed. From near the Riedpass (3565m.) slant up the N flank of the Ulrichshorn, then up its short N ridge ($3\frac{1}{2}$ h.). Now descend the SW ridge to the Windjoch (15 min., $3\frac{3}{4}$ h. from Bordier hut).

104. From the Windjoch climb the snowy NE ridge of the Nadelhorn, easy up to where it narrows and rocks appear. Continue up loose rocks and snow over pt. 4115m. to firm slabby rocks (easy-angled grooves) which lead directly to the summit (2 h.

148

from Windjoch, $3\frac{1}{2}$ h. from Mischabel hut, $5\frac{3}{4}$ h. from Bordier hut).

NADELGRAT

The traverse described below reaches or crosses the Hohberg-horn, Stecknadelhorn, Nadelhorn and Lenzspitze. It is un-questionably one of the finest traverses of its type and class in the Alps. The expedition is better in every way than the Forbes Ridge of the Chardonnet and the Rochefort Ridge in the Mont Blanc Range. It is hard to compare with other traverses in the Zermatt region, but its rocky sections, for example, are easier than the Zinalrothorn and Portjengrat. One ignores the fact that the geographical name of the Nadelgrat does not strictly belong to some parts of the Hohberghorn and Lenz-spitze. The route of the classic traverse adopted by alpinists has earned the right to assume the name which becomes neither more nor less than the ground covered by climbing parties.

Traverse North-South. This is the proper direction, although it is neither more difficult nor less exhilarating in the other. You start and finish at the Dom hut. The ridge is in a magni-ficent position and at an elevation of well over 4000m. An equal amount of climbing on rock, snow or ice. The rock is generally excellent; the snow crests are very narrow, exposed but rarely corniced. A reasonably safe and sure expedition in most con-ditions. Considering its length a competent party can cover the distance in a relatively short time (9 h. for the round trip is commonplace). PD+. First traverse: a party led by Christian Klucker in 1892, although the ridge had been done in two parts on different occasions before this date.

105. From the Dom hut follow Route 95 to the Festijoch ($2\frac{1}{2}$ h.) and continue along this ordinary route to the Dom till you reach c. 3750m. on the Hohberg glacier. Now cross the glacier hori-zontally N and reach the foot of the broad open couloir coming down from the Stecknadeljoch (4142m.), between the Hohberg-horn on the L and Stecknadelhorn on R (45 min.). There is a general area of broken rocks on the L side of this couloir in its lower half. Starting at the R side, climb these rocks near their centre to the snowy upper half, then go straight up the plain slope to the col, all straightforward and fairly steep ($1\frac{1}{4}$ h., $4\frac{1}{2}$ h. or less from Dom hut).

From the col you can climb a broad snow ridge then a few rocks to the top of the Hohberghorn (15 min.). Most parties make this detour to bag a summit. Return to the col (30 min. up and down).

From the Stecknadeljoch a spiky ridge runs to the Stecknadelhorn (4241m.). Climb on the crest and easily avoid teeth and gaps by using a system of ledges a few m. down on the R(S) side. The rocks are quite good but there are loose blocks (30 min.). From the summit descend steep easy rocks to a level snow saddle which is followed towards the Nadelhorn and rocks again. Climb straight up a flattish rock tower on the ridge and down (II) to a snow gap. Now trend a little L of the blunt crest, over wide snow grooves and slabby rocks, to the NE ridge, which leads in a few min. to the top of the Nadelhorn (45 min.).

The ridge now runs SE down to the Nadeljoch (4213m.*). Climb direct over large blocks till you can see down the ridge. It consists of several gendarmes in regular steps. Traverse or turn them (usually on the L) as you wish. There are so many possibilities within a few m. of each other that detailed instructions are unnecessary. Mainly slabs, walls and cracks, all short, it is possible to weave down the ridge never more than 10m. from the crest without exceeding grade II. There are harder pitches if you want them. Arrive all too soon at the rock islands marking the Nadeljoch and the start of the fine snow crest running to the Lenzspitze. This is the most delicate part of the traverse. If the sharp crest has been levelled by previous parties, then it will be crossed quickly. It is usually in two sections with a rock island between; a classical situation.

from Lenzspitze

Nadelhorn

104

105

Stecknadeljoch

Stecknadelhorn

Hohberghorn

105

105

When there is only a little snow near the summit of the Lenz-spitze, you reach the cairn from the L by climbing a crack (II+) in a smooth wall (on average, 45 min.). Now reverse Route 98 or 99 to the Lenzjoch (1 h.) and so back to the Dom hut (2¼ h., about 10¼ h., allow 12 h. for round trip).

STECKNADELHORN 4241m.

A minor summit on the Nadelgrat (see above) between the Nadel-horn and Hohberghorn. Invariably crossed while undertaking the previous route. First ascent: O. Eckenstein with M. Zur-briggen, 8 August, 1887.

STECKNADELJOCH 4142m.

Between the Stecknadelhorn and Hohberghorn. Its S side is the trade route approach to the Nadelgrat (see above). The N side, down to the Ried glacier, is blocked by ice cliffs and has probably never been climbed.

HOHBERGHORN 4219m.

A pleasant snow summit at the NW end of the Nadelgrat. Easily climbed by the approach to the Nadelgrat, as described in Route 105 (about 4½ h. from Dom hut). Normally accepted as a con-solation prize if parties cannot continue the Nadelgrat because of bad conditions or poor weather. PD-.
  First ascent: R. B. Heathcote with F. Biner, P. Perren and P. Taugwalder. August, 1869. First winter ascent: H. Fritsch with O. Supersaxo and G. Imseng, 5 March, 1921.

DÜRRENHORN 4034.9m.

This mtn. is well seen from Zermatt, and in recent years its popularity has been increasing. From the Dom hut it is usually climbed in combination with the Hohberghorn. It can be app-roached directly from the Bordier hut, and from here marks the start of a fine expedition round the head of the Ried glacier

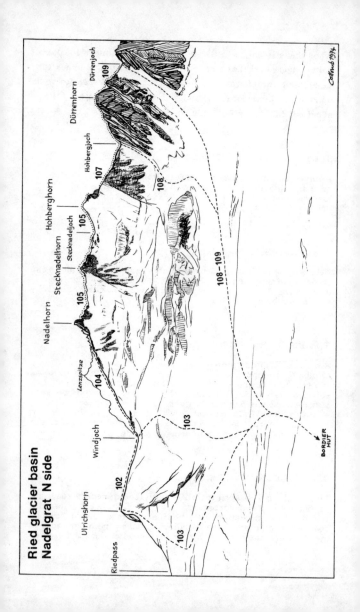

Ried glacier basin
Nadelgrat N side

Riedpass · Ulrichshorn · Windjoch · Lenzspitze · Nadelhorn · Stecknadelhorn · Stecknadeljoch · Hohberghorn · Hohbergjoch · Dürrenhorn · Dürrenjoch

102 · 103 · 104 · 105 · 105 · 107 · 108 · 109 · 108–109

BORDIER HUT

Collins 1974

basin over all the important summits of the Nadelgrat, except the Lenzspitze.

First tourist ascent: A. F. Mummery and W. Penhall with A. Burgener and F. Imseng, 7 September, 1879. First winter ascent, as for Hohberghorn.

From the South (Hohbergjoch). The usual route from the Dom hut. The approach involves a height loss of 250m., after crossing the Festijoch. PD+.

106. From the Dom hut follow Route 95 to the Festijoch and descend to the Hohberg glacier. Now bear L(NW) and go down the glacier (crevasses), then bear R(N) towards the foot of the W spur of the Hohberghorn. Pass this (small icefall just above), then work R towards the rocks (3 h.). Enter the first couloir opening in these (c. 3480m.), running up into the W spur, climb this steep snow couloir for about 60m., then break out L along steep scree or snow ledges and ramps. Follow this line of weakness across ribs and couloirs to the NE and reach a small glacier under the Hohbergjoch. Make a rising traverse in the same direction across the glacier to reach the Hohbergjoch (3916m.) (1½ h.). From the col climb the rocky SE ridge without difficulty to the summit (30 min., 5 h. from Dom hut). The recommended return route is across the Hohberghorn, as described in reverse below.

By traverse of Hohberghorn. An interesting and varied approach to the mtn., as for the Nadelgrat. PD.

107. From the Dom hut follow Route 105 to the summit of the Hohberghorn (4½ h.). Descend the main NNW ridge of this mtn. towards the Dürrenhorn. It starts with a snow crest, ending at the top of a steep step. Either climb straight down (II+, good rock) to easy rocks, or when the snow is good turn the step on the R by a steep slope. Continue down the broad easy snow ridge to some rocks which lead to the saddle of the Hohbergjoch (3916m.) where the previous route is joined. By loose but

155

easy rocks climb the short SE ridge of the Dürrenhorn to its summit (30 min., $5\frac{3}{4}$ h. from Dom hut. 4 h. in reverse by same route).

108. From the Mischabel hut follow Route 102 to the Windjoch ($1\frac{1}{2}$ h.). You can now either make the steep descent (icy) on the other side to the Ried glacier, or climb over the Ulrichshorn to reach the Ried glacier (Routes 102 and 103). Cross the glacier in a curve to the N and SW, turning the base of a rognon at c. 3600m. on its N side to reach the foot of the slope below the Hohbergjoch ($2-3\frac{1}{2}$ h. according to route and conditions). Either climb the broad snow/ice slope of an open couloir to the col 45-50°, or follow the broken rock rib to its R. AD (1 h.). Then up the final ridge as for the previous routes (30 min., $3\frac{1}{2}$-5 h. from Mischabel hut).

109. From the Bordier hut start as for Route 103, and from the vicinity of the Riedpass cross the Ried glacier WSW to the foot of the col. Then as for the route above (about $4\frac{1}{2}$ h. from Bordier hut to summit).

For returning to the Bordier hut you can descend the N ridge of the mtn. to the Dürrenjoch (3860m.), keeping to the crest, short difficulties. From the col go down loose rocks on the L side of the large snow couloir dropping to the Ried glacier. AD.

WINDJOCH 3850m.

Between the Nadelhorn and Ulrichshorn, an important access point to the main ridge of the Mischabel chain. See Routes 102 and 103. First tourist traverse: W. M. Conway, G. Scriven and H. West with J. J. Truffer, A. Zurbrücken and J. Knubel, 30 July, 1886. On ski: Marcel Kurz, W. Odermatt and S. Ehrismann, 27 March, 1912.

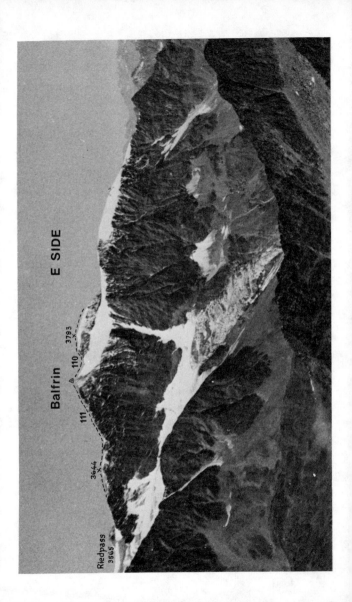

ULRICHSHORN 3925m.

A fine snow summit, frequently climbed. See Routes 102 and 103. First ascent: M. Ulrich and J. J. Imseng with F. Andenmatten, J. Madutz, S. Biner and M. Zumtaugwald, 10 August, 1848. Traversed on ski by Windjoch party two days later.

RIEDPASS 3568m.

Between the Ulrichshorn and Balfrin, a broad snow saddle leading from the Ried glacier to the Bider glacier (Saas valley). Rarely crossed. First traverse by Ulrichshorn party.

BALFRIN 3795.7m.

A mtn. primarily of interest to climbers visiting the Bordier hut. The quickest way of reaching it from the Mischabel hut is to traverse the Ulrichshorn from the Windjoch to the Riedpass (Routes 102 and 103). A traverse is usual from the Bordier hut.
   First ascent: R. S. Watson and Mrs Watson with J. J. Imseng, F. Andenmatten and J. M. Claret, 6 July, 1863.

Gross Bigerhorn and North-West Ridge. By far the most interesting route, at an easy angle and standard. F+. First ascent before 1878.

110. From the Bordier hut descend the hut approach path for a few min., to where the path suddenly drops more steeply. Now slant L across scree, following a line of cairns and track in a small hollow. Later descend a little then go up the lateral moraine of the Ried glacier. A track along the crest leads to the highest point (3084m.) (45 min.). From here climb straight over scree NE to the WSW ridge of the Gross Bigerhorn (3626m.) above, and follow this ridge, blocks and scree, to the top of the latter mtn. (1½ h.). Climb down the snowy ridge towards the Balfrin, over a rocky knoll, to the saddle (3594m.) at the foot of the NW ridge of the NW summit of the Balfrin (3783m.). On

the L of the ridge an easy snow slope leads to this first top (45 min.). Continue down snowy rocks to a gap between the NW summit and the highest point, and reach the latter without difficulty (15 min., $3\frac{1}{4}$ h. from Bordier hut).

South Ridge. Convenient for descent in making a traverse of the mtn. F+. First ascensionists.

111. From the Bordier hut start as for the previous route, to the top of the moraine, from where you follow the Ried glacier route towards the Windjoch. Go up to the snowfields close to the foot of the S ridge and beside the Riedpass. Reach the ridge at a snow shoulder (3644m.) immediately N of this pass ($2\frac{3}{4}$ h.). Climb easy rocks on the ridge to the top (45 min., $3\frac{1}{2}$ h. from Bordier hut, 2 h. in descent).

INDEX OF ROUTES SHOWN ON DIAGRAMS

GENERAL INDEX

165

168